EDDIE O'CONNOR

A dangerous visionary

EDDIE O'CONNOR

A dangerous
visionary

CURRACH
BOOKS

First published in 2021 by

 CURRACHBOOKS

Block 3b, Bracken Business Park, Bracken Road Sandyford
Dublin 18, D18 K277
www.currachbooks.com

ISBN: 978-178218-927-5

Set in Adobe Garamond Pro 11/15
Cover and book design by Alba Esteban | Currach Books
Cover picture by Alexis Sierra
Printed by L&C, Poland

This book is made from Forest Stewardship Council® certified paper

To Hildegarde, Lesley and Robert for their constant support and to my late parents, the brilliant Bob and my mother, Una.

CONTENTS

INTRODUCTION

The atmosphere is accumulating energy at a rate of four Hiroshima-strength atomic bombs every second.

In 2019 a net additional 33 to 36.8 billion tonnes of CO_2 were released into the atmosphere as a result of burning fossil fuels. This has had the effect of causing major social disruption, which has reached devastating levels in some parts of the world. A blatant demonstration of this is Lake Chad in Africa, which is now one tenth the size it was in 1963. The livelihoods of 10.7 million people have been severely disrupted, and in many cases the only source of fresh water has been removed. The Sahara marches southwards as the CO_2 concentration increases. It affects Ghana, the Ivory Coast and other countries in the region, reducing the agricultural potential of huge areas, and forcing internal and some external migration.

Global politics and economics have failed to grasp the enormity and urgency of the need to eliminate the use of fossil fuels. It took the leadership of one Swedish schoolgirl to highlight the foolhardiness of such intransigence to the upcoming generation. Greta Thunberg inspired millions of schoolchildren in more than 110 countries across the world to start striking in protest at the escalating climate crisis. These young people are incredulous that, despite warnings such as that from the UN's leading scientists in 2018 that there were just 12 years left to limit climate catastrophe, their parents' generation seem so resistant to change.

What drives me ultimately is a respect for the environment. We humans have created the Anthropocene, the era in which every aspect of this planet's welfare is influenced by our species. From the Arctic to the Antarctic, and everywhere in between, the hand of human interference with the physical environment is visible. We have transformed the environment and energy is at the centre of this transformation.

We, who have created such comfortable lifestyles for ourselves in the developed world through the use of fossil fuels, know what has to be done and we have the capabilities to do it. If we don't make this one-off transition to sustainability quickly enough, we will destroy the atmosphere for subsequent generations. I have seen an estimate that 6.7 billion people could lose their lives if the greenhouse gas situation is not dealt with.

I started dedicating my working life to decarbonisation more than 30 years ago. A remark made to me in 1989 started me thinking about the threat of global warming. I was chief executive of the Irish government-owned peat company, Bord na Móna (BNM), at the time. One of the board members, Eoin O'Neill, chief technical adviser at the Department of Energy, mentioned how (CO_2), which is released into the atmosphere by burning fossil fuels, absorbs energy. It is one of those 'greenhouse gases' that blocks the escape of heat from the Earth's surface and retains this heat in the atmosphere.

The generation of all electricity at that time, apart from nuclear and hydro, was releasing CO_2. It was shocking for me, in many respects, to realise that I was involved in doing something so damaging, something that was having negative effects on people and on all other species. By 1992, BNM had established its first wind farm, in Oweninny, County Mayo. I could see that wind was a huge resource in Ireland, and capturing it and turning it into electricity made great sense.

When I stepped down from the top job at BNM in 1996, having been embroiled in a bruising, high-profile controversy, it didn't take me long to decide what to do next. Wind energy, I knew, was the way to go.

I founded Future Wind Partnership, which evolved into Airtricity, at a time when people were saying renewable energy was too expensive. I borrowed €25,000 to set it up and got back €48 million when the company was sold in 2008. I ploughed €32 million of that into Mainstream, which has become a global leader in the development of wind and solar plants. Now my passion is directed towards the 'Supergrid', which Europe needs if it is to move to 100% renewable energy.

In February 2020, UN Secretary General Antonio Gutteres issued a statement to the effect that the rise in temperature that was attributable to the build-up of greenhouse gases in the atmosphere was going to exceed the 2-degree limit enshrined by the Paris Accord in 2015. Five years after that agreement, the world continues to heap more greenhouse gases into the atmosphere each year.

In the three years prior to 2020 some $2.5 trillion was invested in new coal-burning plant. JP Morgan, one of the principal funders of this new investment into coal, rounds on its detractors and says that the climate-concerned folk are selfish and want to condemn the rest of humanity to continued poverty. 'We supply heat and light to people who haven't got it at the moment,' JP Morgan proclaims self-righteously.

A recent Greenpeace Asia report collated the damage caused by burning fossil fuels. Each year 4.5 million people die of diseases caused mainly by burning coal, but diesel fumes also contribute. There is a real cost of $2.9 trillion to the people of the world. These facts are not the spurious outpourings of climate alarmists, so called by Donald Trump and his acolytes in Australia, and JP Morgan and others who put greed before their children's futures.

The 25,000 homes that were destroyed by uncontrollable bush and forest fires in Australia have to be paid for by someone. Forests along the whole west coast of the US and Canada have been burning for the past five years. According to a Bloomberg estimate, the cost of the California fires ran to $24.5 billion in 2019. People in Florida are having to relocate to higher ground because of rising sea levels. All insurance premiums have become more expensive because of the additional costs of climate-induced damage.

On a lighter note, the huge growth in the English wine industry is attributable to the fact that the temperature as far north as Norwich is the same as it was in Champagne in the 1980s. The Merlot grape, which accounts for 66% of the wine made in Bordeaux, now ripens completely, making wine with an alcoholic strength of almost 16%, and will have to be replaced by vines that are more accustomed to heat.

Global warming is changing everything. If there was ever a cause that affected all citizens, it is this forced alteration in the climate.

We rightly identified the coronavirus as a threat and took extraordinary actions, as individuals, communities and governments, to cope with it. A far more violent and intractable issue is that of global warming. If, and indeed when, the coronavirus returns we will have a vaccine or medicines to help cope with it. There is no vaccine to deal with global warming. The only cure is a change in human behaviour.

Why are we not honouring the Paris Accord? I believe there are three reasons why humans continue to behave self-destructively.

The first reason is vested interests. The oil, gas and coal businesses spend a fortune pulling the wool over people's eyes. We have BP alleging, ludicrously, that BP stands for 'beyond petroleum', and saying that they are going to decarbonise the production of oil. This is like taking out 100 units of CO_2 so that profits can be made from the 1,000 million units that will be released. Shell has almost convinced the world that natural gas is practically renewable. They can say this because natural gas can be turned into electricity more efficiently than coal. What remains unsaid is that some 40% of natural gas escapes into the atmosphere at the mining and transportation stages, with a far greater effect on climate than that of CO_2. Exxon and Chevron have spent $3.5 billion on public relations in their attempt to convince populations that oil and gas are good for you.

The second reason is ignorance. This applies to politicians as much as it does to ordinary folk. In Ireland we had one of the Healy-Raes claiming in the Dáil that God was responsible for global warming. Even the Taoiseach remarked that global warming wasn't all downside, as it meant that people didn't have to pay so much to heat their houses. Like natural gas, CO_2 is colourless, odourless and of itself non-toxic, and the atmosphere appears infinite. Besides, we breathe it out with every breath. How can CO_2, which we exhale, be harmful?

Global warming exposes the soft underbelly of democracy. Almost all elected politicians lead from behind. According to former Longford-Westmeath TD Henry Abbott, the art of being a politician is knowing where the people are at and being one millimetre behind them. There are few enough statesmen or stateswomen. Of course, democracy trumps autocracy, communism, rule by oligarchs, or regency, but it sometimes fails when dealing with mass ignorance. Jean-Claude Juncker, former President of the EU Commission, has said 'We know what has to be done [to combat climate change], only we don't know how to get elected when we have done it.' Explaining that wind and solar were cheaper than coal and gas would surely go a long way to helping the voting public understand the reasoning behind proposed CO_2 reduction measures

The third reason is bad policy formulation. What does this mean? Electrical utility companies have known for some time now that renewable energy is cheaper than coal-, oil- or gas-fired energy.

Coal-fired plant costs in the order of 9 $ cents per unit of electricity over the lifetime of the plant, whereas wind and solar energy lie in a range of one third to three quarters of this price. However, this comparison does not deal with like for like.

Wind and solar don't pollute, fossils do. The current cost to the world of burning fossils is an extra $79 for each tonne of CO_2 released, which equates to another 7 $ cents on top of the 9 $ cents nominal charge per unit of electricity.

Why have the Kyoto Protocol and the Paris Accord failed? Nobel laureate William Nordhaus, in a very well-written piece in the journal *Foreign Affairs*, explains that both agreements relied on voluntary commitments from participating countries. The US and Canada pulled out of the Kyoto Protocol early on in the Bush administration and it was let slide into oblivion in 2012. Paris is going the same way. Since 2015, when the Accord was agreed, the quantity of greenhouse gases in the atmosphere has increased every year, and not by a trivial amount.

There are no penalties for nations that increase their output of greenhouse gases. Thus, Trump was able to pull out of the Paris Accord without any consequences. Even though the US continues to close its coal-fired electricity generating plant, and is among the leading nations for installing wind and solar, the signal given out by the US departure from the Paris Accord was picked up globally, allowing countries like Australia, Russia and Saudi Arabia to continue with carbon-creating industries with the excuse that the second-largest carbon emitter had abandoned Paris.

The election of Joe Biden to the presidency of the US in 2020 was truly significant in the struggle to contain climate change. There was no behind-the-scenes politicking involved in his commitment to reducing CO_2 emissions. He made it an election issue, bringing it up in the televised debates with Donal Trump, and declaring climate change to be the 'number one issue facing humanity'. He promised a national transition from fossil fuels to renewable energy, which he says will create millions of new jobs. Biden has a $2 trillion plan that puts the US on a path to zero carbon pollution from the electricity sector by 2035 and net-zero emissions by 2050. At the UN in October 2020, Chinese premier Xi Jinping declared that China would be completely decarbonised by 2060, and this was immediately followed with similar declarations by Korea and Japan.

Nordhaus, however, argues that the architecture of the Paris Accord is wrong and that it is doomed as a result.

> Since they are directed at a hard problem, international climate agreements start with an incentive structure that has proved intrinsically difficult to make work. They have also been undermined by myopic or venal leaders who have no interest in long-term global issues and refuse to take the problem seriously. Further obstacles are the scale, difficulty, and cost of slowing climate change.
>
> But in addition to facing the intrinsic difficulty of solving the hard problem of climate change, international climate agreements have been based on a flawed model of how they should be structured. The central flaw has been to overlook the incentive structure. Because countries do not realistically appreciate that the challenge of global warming presents a prisoner's dilemma, they have negotiated agreements that are voluntary and promote free-riding—and are thus sure to fail.[1]

He argues that when one country or continent cuts greenhouse gas emissions, and the result benefits the whole world, countries

---

[1]   William Nordhaus, 'The Climate Club: How to fix a Failing Global Effort', *Foreign Affairs*, May/June 2020.

that have done nothing get a free ride. These countries are then incentivised to continue polluting as others do the right thing.

> Suppose that when Country A spends $100 on abatement, global damages decline by $200 but Country A might get only $20 worth of the benefits: its national cost-benefit analysis would lead it not to undertake the abatement. Hence, nations have a strong incentive not to participate in such agreements. The outcome is a noncooperative free-riding equilibrium, in which few countries undertake strong climate change policies—a situation that closely resembles the current international policy environment.

> When it comes to climate change policies today, nations speak loudly but carry no stick at all.[2]

Nordhaus proposes that a club of nations be set up to put a price on greenhouse gas emissions, a carbon price. This carbon price acts as a strong and sufficient incentive on all sections of the club's membership to change their polluting behaviours. Non-members would have tariffs imposed on all goods and services sold into member countries.

The carbon price needs to be motivational, to act as a strong incentive to companies, governments and households to change their behaviours. It has been proved in the past that Sulphur (SOX) emissions from power stations can be almost eliminated by the imposition of a sufficient price (tax). A similar result can be achieved with an adequate carbon price.

I imagine that at the next meeting of the COP, this reasoning will be taken on board. This meeting, which was due to take place in Glasgow in December 2020, was postponed due to the Covid-19 pandemic.

---

2   Ibid.

One effect of the failure of the Paris Accord is a semi-bankrupt wind turbine and solar manufacturing industrial sector. The profitability of wind turbine manufacturing is a collective zero. The original equipment suppliers (OEMs) receive no reward for the innovations that have seen turbines move from being small esoteric luxuries, beloved of environmental NGOs, to being super-efficient power stations.

Vast sums have been invested by the likes of Vestas, Siemens Gamesa, Nordex, Acciona, Goldwind and GE in improving the economics of wind energy. Each new generation of wind turbines costs the company in the order of €400 to €500 million. Markets are aware of this innovation, and disapprove of it. In the recent past Siemens Gamesa announced that they were developing a 15MW turbine for the offshore. Their share price reduced by 5%. Energy companies that improve their product offering, thereby reducing the price of electricity, should be rewarded by investors; instead they are penalised. There is, however, a certain logic to this. Investors know that there is no market mechanism that will reward the added investment. In the next round of auctions for offshore contracts all the benefits of Siemens Gamesa's investments will be passed on to the electricity customer.

New renewable energy-generation plant is awarded by regulators through auctions. These auctions are based only on price. This price results from competition and is independent of the value created by making electricity that doesn't pollute. Every unit of electricity that is made from fossil fuels has a pollution price tag of 7 $ cents associated with it. This is calculated by referring to the global cost of greenhouse gas pollution ($2.9 trillion per annum), and dividing this by tonnes of gases emitted (36 billion).

Developers of wind and solar plant, along with the original equipment manufacturers and the myriad service suppliers, are paid only for the electricity produced. Each unit of electricity mitigates a definite amount of CO_2. They are not paid for this mitigation. All the benefit of the wind turbine company's investment flows to the electricity customer. There can be no clearer example of policy failure than this mechanical application of lowest price allocation of renewable energy contracts. Put simply, the wind companies are doing the right thing, and they are penalised for this.

In contrast, oil and gas companies make around 20% from upstream activities. It is no wonder that very few investments into renewables are made by oil and gas companies. As recently as October 2019, JP Morgan recommended that no one should invest in renewable energy – oil and gas were the way to go if you wanted to maximise your returns.

The perverse nature of lowest price auctions means that the main tool for reversing global warming – doing away with fossil fuel electricity production – is penalised and discouraged. Investment flows to sectors in which it is possible to make a return. There is massive under-investment in the transition to renewable energy, probably a quarter to a fifth of what it needs to be to halt the seemingly inexorable rise in greenhouse gas emissions.

In the wind turbine manufacturing industry, there have been significant forced mergers and acquisitions as well as bankruptcies. Renewable manufacturing plant is being closed down at a time when companies should be incentivised to increase production.

The bad architecture of the Paris Accord induces the kind of policy failure we are witnessing now. Wind turbine manufacturing companies are forced to supply turbines below their real cost, while the oil and gas companies continue to extract oil and gas at relatively high profit. It is to be hoped that the delayed Glasgow COP meeting will completely change the philosophy underlying the next international climate-saving agreement.

It must be a source of worry to all concerned citizens as to why Trump pulled the US out of the Paris Accord. There are probably two reasons why he ignored best scientific advice and removed the US from Paris.

The US Republican Party is firmly in the clutches of the big oil and gas companies, in particular Exxon and Chevron, although it is known that Shell, BP and others also contribute to the party (but most of them gave to the Democrats too). It has been stated, without refutation, that the oil and gas companies collectively have spent $3.5 billion in the past 10 years on public relations and on paying senators and members of Congress to represent their interests. These companies and the Koch brothers (who own coal mines) donated large amounts to Trump's election campaign in 2016. They were pushing an open door when they prevailed on Trump to abandon the Paris climate process.

Trump's mother was Scottish and he was inveigled by Alex Salmond, the Scottish First Minister, into investing in Scotland. In 2006 he acquired some 1,400 acres in Balmedie, north of Aberdeen, with the intention of building a massive golf resort there. He proposed to build two 18-hole golf courses, a 450-room hotel, conference centre and spa, 36 golf villas, 950 holiday homes, accommodation for 400 staff and residential developments comprising 500 houses. According to an analysis by Scottish Natural Heritage this would substantially damage the wildlife habitats at a Site of Special Scientific Interest (SSSI).

The construction of the golf course was finished in 2012. The only way to make money out of golf courses is by selling off the plots adjacent to the golf course, those designated for villas and holiday homes. Sales of these plots were going slowly. Trump, as is his wont, was casting around for someone besides himself to blame. He discovered that planning permission had been given for a 92MW wind farm in the sea, a few kilometres from the coast. It is a kind of test site for offshore turbines. Nothing was built there until 2017, but in 2013 Trump started a campaign to have the wind farm stopped. He wrote 18 abusive letters to Salmond, and challenged the wind farm planning decision through every possible court, up to the Supreme Court, losing every case.

Trump got the central part of his commercial planning wrong. It is hard to see why people would build holiday homes so far north in Scotland. In addition, there are a large number of excellent golf courses in the vicinity of Edinburgh Airport, much closer than Aberdeen for visiting Americans who would be the principal investors targeted by Trump.

CHAPTER 1

Childhood

I grew up listening to stories of the incredible courage of my father, Robert (Bob) O'Connor. Anybody who gets to be called an entrepreneur has to have a few things going for them and one is not being afraid to do things. Well, you might be afraid but, to coin the title of US psychologist Susan Jeffers's best-selling book, you should *Feel the Fear and Do It Anyway*. My father forged a public service career in education, official statistics and economics. His philosophy throughout was that you work hard to discover facts – and they may not always be obvious – and then you're not afraid to call it as you see it. What really used to annoy him was people who pulled their punches; advisers who would write a paper, giving the facts that pointed to a certain way forward but, because a politician said something contrary, they wouldn't be forthright about the conclusions. He couldn't stand that; he was dedicated to facts and reality – not to form but to content. He wasn't afraid to stay true to his research findings even when they weren't popular and conflicted with official pronouncements. That was the sort of excitement, sometimes bordering on anger, that I was brought up on.

One of eight children in a dirt-poor farming family, Bob was born in the townland of Leitrim, near Frenchpark in County Roscommon, a week before the Easter Rising of 1916. I remember his mother, Granny O'Connor, as a small, bent old lady with a stick who told me how her marriage had been arranged. She was simply told, 'Here's your husband'; he was 'that wee man with the cap'. That was how things were done then in rural Ireland; matches were made, often with an eye to farm alliances, and few marriages were founded on love stories. I can remember my other granny (Rushe) saying that 'this love thing' was grossly overrated.

Talk about changing cultures. I suppose every generation sees a lot of change in their lifetime but I think we have seen more than most.

My father didn't do the Leaving Certificate and would never have gone to college but for the encouragement of his wonderful sister Molly, who was a teacher. And while his family would have found it near impossible to fund his third-level education, he was a bright student who won scholarships. In 1935 the Roscommon County Committee of Agriculture awarded him a scholarship to go to the Albert Agricultural College in Glasnevin, Dublin. After a year there, he sat a state scholarship exam to study agricultural science at University College Dublin and was one of four students to be awarded funding by the Department of Agriculture.

While in college he captained the boxing team that won the Irish Intervarsity Championship in 1940. He also played every year on the college's Gaelic football team that competed for the Sigerson Cup – the premier championship among higher education institutions. After leaving UCD in the summer of 1940 with an honours BAgSc, he got a job back in County Roscommon, teaching rural science in Ballaghaderreen Vocational School.

The vocational schools were less academic than other second-level schools, teaching subjects such as farm skills, commerce and shorthand and typing.

Two years later he was appointed headmaster of the new Vocational School in Elphin, County Roscommon, and in 1946 he married Una Rushe, whose family lived just outside the town. One of her brothers, Des, was an influential theatre critic and columnist with the *Irish Independent* from the 1960s to the 1990s. I think my parents probably met through GAA football at a time when the county was on a high with their team's success. Roscommon were back-to-back All-Ireland champions in 1943 and 1944; I know my father was a very enthusiastic supporter and I am sure my mother was a team groupie. She had attended the Mercy Convent in Roscommon and worked in various menial or clerical jobs after school. She was employed as a secretary in the law firm of solicitor Jack Kelly in Elphin at one time.

I was their first child, born on 26 June 1947, just 10 months after their wedding, followed by my brother Desmond, less than two years later, on 4 April 1949. It must have been very hard on my mother when my father headed off to study in the US at Iowa State University at Ames in June 1950, leaving her with two very young children. This opportunity to go to Ames arose after my father completed a MAgSc, for which he had carried out a financial survey of 20 cattle farms in the Elphin area in 1945/46. The results were published in a paper that he read to the Statistical and Social Inquiry Society of Ireland in 1948. His findings caused considerable controversy at the time because they showed very low incomes in all the farms surveyed. It was not the sort of downbeat news the first inter-party government wanted to hear in the year that the 26 counties were officially declared the Republic of Ireland. Minister for Agriculture James Dillon, when questioned in the Dáil about the figures, tried to discredit them by declaring that 'The farmers stuck their fingers in the author's eye deliberately and persistently.' Yet, when my father repeated the exercise on 25 farms in mid-Roscommon two years later, he got similar results.

After my father's address to the Statistical and Social Inquiry Society, he was approached by the US agricultural attaché to Ireland, Joe Corrigan, who suggested he look for funding to study in the US through the Marshall Aid Plan – a $13 billon programme set up in 1948 to provide economic assistance to European countries to help them rebuild after the Second World War. He studied economic statistics and mathematics at graduate level in Iowa for a year but, under the terms of the Marshall Plan, he wasn't allowed to take a degree there. However, on his return to Ireland he worked on a thesis about factors affecting the supply of pigs in Ireland and this was accepted for a PhD from UCD.

It's difficult now to envisage the level of poverty in Ireland in the late 1940s and early 1950s when emigration was rampant. Yet all I remember is happiness. I started school with the nuns in Elphin, but then we moved to Dublin in 1954, after my father was headhunted by the director of the Central Statistics Office (CSO), Dr R. C. Geary, to lead the first National Farm Income Survey, which began in 1955. It was a huge undertaking in those days, involving 2,000 farms around the country, and again, when they were published in September 1956, the results gave rise to much disquiet in political and administrative circles. Apart from dairy farms, the incomes were abysmally low and exploded the long-held view in urban areas that farmers were rolling in wealth.

We lived on Anne Devlin Road in one of Dublin's expanding suburbs, Templeogue, for just two years before we moved north when my father was appointed chief administrative officer of Monaghan Vocational Education Committee (VEC). Monaghan is full of hills and is an ideal setting for a wild kind of childhood. My brother and I went to CBS in Monaghan town – on top of a hill – and I learned how to defend myself there. I remember being given a hard time as an 'outsider' coming to the town; you had to become very tough. Overall, though, I recall it as a time of great freedom; I had no sense of danger and was allowed to be a child. Through my father's job I had access to a carpentry workshop where I loved to make arrows. It was an idyllic time.

One of the things I recall was being brought fishing on one of the many lakes in Castleblayney, where we caught pike and perch. That was very exciting. Although Bob really didn't have the patience for rod fishing, those trips and fishing in the convent lake in Monaghan gave me a lifelong interest in, indeed a passion for fishing.

Two years later the family was uprooted again when my father was offered a permanent job in the CSO. Although it carried a much higher salary than his VEC post, he was sorry to be leaving Monaghan so soon. For me it felt very disruptive, continuing a pattern of getting comfortable with friends in places and then you're gone, never to see them again, except for a few during my university years. I remember the late Frank McCormack in Elphin with particular fondness.

I think moving house a number of times had a big influence on my life. I imagine it made me a bit more self-contained, but how can anybody be objective about which childhood events had a formative effect? It was just something I had to cope with. I always had an individualistic streak, driven by what could be achieved. From an early age, I tended to see a bigger picture and perhaps it was one that was more distorted than that of the guys around me.

In 1958, I went to Oatlands Primary School, an all-boys' CBS in Stillorgan, for a year. But my father was keen that my brother and myself would get scholarships to secondary school so he sent us to Kilmacud National School, which had a great reputation for successfully preparing pupils for scholarship exams. It worked for my brother but not for me.

My parents then decided it would be best if I was sent away to the Cistercian College in Roscrea, County Tipperary, a private boarding school. The one thing I remember about the preparations for that was the purchase of a silver napkin ring that I needed for use in the dining room. However, an injury to my left arm during the summer of 1960 scuppered those plans. I had to have surgery at Our Lady's Hospital for Sick Children in Crumlin to remove a chip off the bone. I still wasn't eating a fortnight after the operation and a serious infection at the site of an injection into my gluteus maximus muscle was discovered, necessitating the draining of a huge amount of pus. I remember, after a period of near starvation, I couldn't get enough food, which seemed to fuel a growth spurt. Weeks later, as I was walking down the road near our home on St Helen's Road, Booterstown, the other elbow began to click and ache. I was taken back to the orthopaedic surgeon, Gerry Brady, who diagnosed a loose cartilage, requiring another operation.

By this stage I reckon my parents thought I was too weak to be sent away so, with the help of the headmaster in Kilmacud National School, they got me into the private Blackrock College just up the road. Dessie, who was quieter and more academic, did go to boarding school two years later, having won a scholarship to De La Salle in Waterford.

Blackrock College, founded by the Holy Ghost Fathers in 1860, became associated with the Catholic Nationalist movement, which dominated political and social thinking in the country almost up to the end of the 1950s. The future Catholic Archbishop of Dublin, John Charles McQuaid, was a president at the college, and formed a close alliance with past pupil and former teacher Éamon de Valera. McQuaid is believed to have had considerable influence on the drafting of the Irish Constitution in 1937 when de Valera was Taoiseach.[1]

I remember I was in the 2B1 class for French and Latin, which was a bit of a comedown. I don't believe in streaming but it certainly motivated me hugely. I knew I was better than that, and by the end of the year I was in the A class. Although Blackrock is a school renowned for rugby and is the alma mater of many former Irish internationals, such as Fergus Slattery, Brendan Mullin and Brian O'Driscoll, I wasn't interested in it then. I played soccer and loved it but I was not particularly good. Unusually, perhaps, it was not

---

1   Father Michael O'Carroll, 'Inspired Educator and Ecumenist of Sorts', in *Studies*, Vol. 87, No. 348.

until during and after university that I was to take up rugby and only then did I develop a passion for the game.

No one can recall their teenage days without the bitter-sweet feeling of regret and delight. It was the headmaster of another school (Mr Potts in Gonzaga) who pointed out to me when my own son was seeking admission there that for a while boys make an exit from the human species and come to resemble rats more than humans. However, with good, supportive education, they re-enter humankind again some time around the age of 18. Certainly my first couple of years in Blackrock were fantastic, then the hormones struck. Until I read Gail Sheehy's book *Passages* many years later, I always thought that what I had gone through was somehow exceptional. She described exactly and precisely what I had experienced. She said the deeper the passage you go through the more perfect the transition. You are a child up to that time, running around kicking football and with no interest in girls or women. At the age of 14 girls suddenly become women and want nothing to do with boys, who just want to mess about with a ball and talk rubbish.

The Lycett girls lived down the road and I remember both Mary and Geraldine each being just like 'one of the boys' in our group of friends. However, one afternoon we were sitting around talking as usual when one of them looked at me and said with great disdain, 'What would you know about that?' I don't believe I spoke to her again after that – or at least she never spoke to me. We had nothing to do with them from then on; we went our way and the girls went theirs.

My classmates at Blackrock were a reflection of societal culture at that time. Only one boy in my class was the son of a big businessman, the rest were sons of civil servants, lawyers, doctors and farmers. That was the early 1960s, during the first programme for economic expansion, when Ireland languished at the bottom of every league table of industrialised countries. Tariff barriers, a relic of the Great Depression, still existed, and the free trade area with Britain came about only in 1965, the year I left Blackrock College.

I remember the study of maths at school as being a very serious affair. It was accepted then that maths was necessary for every form of thinking profession, perhaps with the exception of law. I didn't find maths easy and spent an hour studying that one subject most nights but I was delighted to have a good grounding in it when I went on to study engineering.

I am sure I was pressured by my father to do engineering or science because I liked building things. I always wanted to know how and why you do things. I remember he brought me for aptitude testing to a psychologist in UCD who reckoned I would be fine to do anything except architecture. My spatial awareness, apparently, wasn't on a par with my other abilities.

My father would have talked a lot about economics and politics at home. During the early 1960s, his role at the CSO involved him in preparing the agricultural output projections for the government's Second Programme for Economic Development in 1963. He looked back on it as 'exacting, difficult and very pressurised' work. 'There were constant demands for more, better and more up-to-date statistics and considerable criticism from government departments if the published results fell short of government plans.' He was relieved to get out of the CSO in 1967 when he was appointed research professor at the Economic and Social Research Institute.

Dessie and I had two sisters: Mary, who was five years younger than me, and Anne, who was born when I was 17. My mother had had three miscarriages and was 45 when she gave birth to Anne; it was like starting a new family. I had an extremely close relationship with my mother until about the age of 11, when, as is normal, I started the slow process of growing away. After that, I always thought that she was hyper-critical of me in every way.

I also remember arguing with my father a lot. My mother would get annoyed and come in with what I regarded as ridiculous comments, not even worthy of acknowledgement, as I got on with denouncing my father. That's all normal healthy stuff for teenagers; I went through that with my own children.

I think the reason that so many terrific businessmen and artists, crusaders and poets emanated from Blackrock College was partly due to the sense of freedom that the teaching staff and the culture of the school instilled. Having worked all my life since with men who were educated in other schools, I think Blackrock was less prescriptive than most. Even though its fame rested on its achievements on the rugby field, at least to the casual observer, there was huge encouragement for all sporting, social and academic activities in the college.

Freedom is a very modern concept. The French Revolution and the US Constitution enshrine it as the founding construct. The Blackrock College of my day practised it. I reckon it was great preparation for university where there was no obligation to study. I suppose the best thought that comes to mind from my years at Blackrock is that the teachers and priests respected you enough to give you the freedom to grow. You were given strong values but in a supportive way, which meant you didn't automatically reject them and they stuck for life.

Even during my school years, it suited my personality to question things, looking for the underlying reality. Why are you here and what are you doing? What is your role in the world and how can you change it? As I see it, these are the fundamental questions in life.

I remember, for instance, studying the Doppler effect during physics classes in fifth year, when we had a hopeless science teacher. The Doppler effect is a noticeable change in the frequency of sound, light or water waves as an object moves towards or away from you in space.

'Why would that be?' I asked the teacher.

'It is to do with pressure,' he replied.

'There's nothing in space, it can't be to do with pressure,' I pointed out.

'Who told you that?' he retorted.

I didn't ask him any more questions after that because I knew he couldn't answer them. I found that with a lot of teachers when I asked fundamental (for me) things. The debates with my father would have been a constant questioning of what was fair.

I was about 13 when I asked my father: 'How do you think?' It was many years later before I really found out the answer to that. He laughed and said you just do.

You have to study and worry about a topic, find out everything you can about it, analyse it to hell and back and then let the sub-conscious take over. I discovered this in my first job, with the ESB. Whenever I came across an intractable technical or engineering problem I would go off and do something like rugby training, come in the next morning and the answer would be there – without any further conscious thought; it is the subconscious at work.

CHAPTER 2

Working at the ESB

I had been president of the students' representative council in UCD in the troubled 1968/69 period, and my reputation preceded me into the workplace. This became apparent after I applied for, and got, a trainee placement at the state Electricity Supply Board (ESB) in 1970.

John Lang, an engineer who was on the interview panel, later told me that the company's accountants didn't want to hire me. They probably regarded my politics as suspect and saw me as a liability. Lang was told: 'If you want to recruit him and take him on, he is your responsibility.'

I had already applied for various positions in Britain, because chemical engineering jobs were very hard to find in Ireland at the time. The big chemical companies, such as BP and Shell, were all based abroad and I would gladly have emigrated if I had got a job.

However, the ESB was growing dramatically at the start of the 1970s and had an intake of about 22 into the generation side of the business. We were put through a very good, well-structured, year-long training programme. I joined in September 1970 and the training started in October. I was immediately sent up to Gweedore, in the heart of the Donegal Gaeltacht. There was a tiny, sod peat-fired power station there and I am sure they loved this callow young man, straight out of college, arriving up from Dublin. There were 70 people employed in the little 5MW station.

At that time Hildegarde (my future wife) was teaching in a secondary school in Bundoran, County Donegal, about 100 kilometres south of Gweedore, and she was living in her native Sligo. So, this posting to the rural north-west wasn't too much of a hardship. I stayed in a guest house for the duration of that training stint. I would hitch a lift down to Sligo on Friday and stay with Hildegarde for the weekend.

I had met Hildegarde while we were both studying in UCD. She was doing an Arts degree and we were both interested in student politics. She lived in various flats near UCD, which at the time was spread out around the centre of Dublin.

Up in Donegal you get a view of traditional Irish culture that you just don't see in Dublin. People in Dublin have no idea that that culture still exists. I found it fascinating then – and still do. It was there I met John Gillespie. I would return to him many years later for Airtricity.

After the training programme I was allocated as a shift engineer at the Pigeon House in Ringsend, Dublin. It got its name from John Pidgeon,[2] the caretaker of a mid-eighteenth-century storehouse, who started to sell refreshments to passengers on the 'packet ships' arriving and departing nearby. In 1793, many years after Pidgeon's death, a hotel was built on the storehouse site to accommodate packet ship passengers.

More than a century later the hotel was converted into a power station that first generated electricity in July 1903 and was run by the Dublin Corporation Lighting Committee.[3] I remember there was a stone plaque outside commemorating councillors who were members of the Lighting Committee, some of whom were mentioned in *Ulysses*, James Joyce's novel set over 24 hours in Dublin on 16 June 1904. The ESB was founded in 1927 and took over the

2   Dublincity.ie
3   Esbarchives.ie

Pigeon House in 1929. The site continued to supply most of the capital's electricity until the 1950s. The ESB had been set up two years after the Irish government had approved the building of an electric power station at Ardnacrusha, County Clare, to harness the River Shannon. It was thought at the time that this would replace the power stations.

When I got into the Pigeon House in 1971 it was ancient and creaking. All of the wise saws in the company laughed at its inefficiency. The new Poolbeg generating station, named after the Poolbeg lighthouse situated at the entrance to Dublin Port, was being built beside it, and the Pigeon House was near the end of its operating life, firing heavy fuel oil – the dirtiest of the dirty. I was the only shift engineer in there and I worked days, but they were long days. There was a shortage of plant at the time as electricity demand was growing by 10% a year and they couldn't build new generation plant fast enough to meet the unprecedented demand. Charlie Murtagh was my boss, a great guy.

It was there I began to learn about industrial relations. I found out that the workers had not even a smidgen of interest in Communism or anything to do with the proletariat. Instead I discovered that the lads had a phenomenal interest in their wage packets. They used to come into my office and ask me to explain to them why the wage packet was as it was. I rapidly had to learn how they were paid and, more importantly, how to explain it to them.

I started teaching them about the theory of the power station. I was trying to make them understand what they were doing. Tony Ryder was a brilliant guy there at the time and he went on to be one of the first four worker-directors appointed by the ESB in 1979.

I learned to handle industrial relations with shop stewards. In the main I liked the interaction with the workers in the station. We didn't do much innovation as trainees, rather we were learning the ropes, learning about safety and learning about people.

There were no real shift workers in the Pigeon House as we were only required during the day, when the demand for electricity was at its highest. I used to have to work two peaks, the morning peak and evening peak, as there was a great shortage of electricity. The demand for electricity goes down overnight and ramps up very quickly in the morning. You are there trying to guide the whole thing, but there were, of course, rules governing how workers were employed. The shift had to be staffed by three people and sometimes a guy would call in sick, so then you would have to call in his mate and get him brought in by taxi and he'd get an overtime payment.

I remember one particular Saturday when Joe Duff was the charge hand, the guy working and supervising the shift workers. Joe was crotchety and I think we had to get 60MW for a peak in the middle of a day. We didn't normally work on Saturday as demand was usually low. However, on this particular Saturday plant had broken down elsewhere and the Pigeon House was needed. We had to get it done and I had to send out for people as it wasn't expected. I was supposed to have five people and I had only three. I remember calling Joe into the office.

'We have a problem here,' I told him.

'You don't have enough staff,' he pointed out, matter-of-factly.

'Joe, I have done my best, I have sent out for them and I just can't find them. You know I would have them all in here if I could; I am not trying to pull one over on you.'

'You've no staff … ,' he repeated.

'We'll have to talk about this, Joe,' I said, hauling out a pint bottle of Guinness – colloquially known as a Danno.

We sat down and shared a Danno of stout – completely against the rules. But afterwards he said, 'You'll have your load'. Joe worked hard that day in the engine room. The union agreement was that there should have been five staff but there were only three, so Joe knew he would be working hard. We got it done and we managed to meet the demand.

He got a terrible slagging from the lads later. 'He bought you off ,Joe,' they said. But we got our load, we made it, whatever it took. I never fell out with Joe. I did fall out with other guys as they would misunderstand something and get excited in themselves. That happened – it was a very family atmosphere in there, very tight, all kinds of different personalities.

I ended up being in the Pigeon House for about four years.

Meeting the peak load required six boilers to be fired up, which involved a lot of manual work. Oil had to be heated, otherwise it wouldn't flow; the oil was then pumped and as it flowed it atomised, turning into tiny droplets that could easily go on fire. The air was fanned into the system and a spark got a flame going. Each boiler heated up and started making steam which was piped to steam turbines. The steam got hotter and hotter, meaning it contained more energy. This heat and pressure energy was turned into rotating energy, which was turned into electrical energy in a generator. The control room operators would tell the operating staff how much electricity to make. The amount of electricity that the station produced was dictated by the central dispatch office, whose job it was to match what was generated with the national customer demand.

The steam, when it had done its work in the turbine, was condensed by water coming in from the Liffey.

The amount of oil that was burned determined the amount of electricity produced. Efficiency is a measure of the amount of energy that is in the oil, which comes out the far end as electricity. As the plant was so old the Pigeon House was at the bottom of every efficiency league, with only about 20% of the oil's energy being converted to electricity.

In 1975 I went to the Ringsend power station, which had been built in 1955, as assistant maintenance engineer. This was a disgracefully run power station at the time, with even worse dysfunctionality than I encountered when I went to BNM as managing director years later. While the Pigeon House had vast limitations because of its age, it was a nice power station with a pleasant boss who had a good sense of humour. Charlie Murtagh was a lovely fellow, with no career aspirations to be CEO or anything. He saw his job as coming into work every day and getting on with people – and he loved painting the place.

In contrast, the Ringsend station was a disaster. There were very bad practices and bad plant; it was breaking down all the time and the safety procedures were terrible. At the time I didn't realise the importance of this because the boss didn't care. He came in at 10am and left at noon, then came back at 2pm and left at 4pm. The standards of management were really horrifying at this much bigger station, which had a generating capacity of 270MW – compared to a capacity of 90MW at the Pigeon House. There was both an A and B station in Ringsend, with much older machinery in the A. Although there were three newer generators in the B station, they gave trouble from day one. As well as having bad management, it was an unlucky station.

I was assistant to Helmut John Stieber, the maintenance superintendent and a fellow engineer. His father, a chemical engineer, had come to Ireland in the 1930s from the Sudetenland. Helmut was sent back to boarding school in Germany in 1939 and ended up being conscripted into the Hitler Youth and fighting on the Eastern Front in the Second World War.

Helmut had very difficult people working for him in Ringsend. There were two of them and, as far as I could see, they did very little. The problem with people who do little work is that they don't want anybody else to do anything either.

When the top boss is dysfunctional everybody is dysfunctional. The place just didn't work at all, not a single element of it; there was no work ethic and the unions ran riot.

Demarcation was rampant – whose job was it to do what? A large, broken 80kW electric motor sat on the floor for about five years. Electricians worked on motors up to 80kW and fitters worked on motors above 80kW, but who was going to work on the one 80kW motor? If you gave it to one lot, you'd have a strike on your hands, and if you gave it to the other lot, ditto. This is the scenario I was sent into.

Helmut never prioritised, he just did everything. There was a German thoroughness about him. He left me to manage the supervisors who kept the place running. They were the most victimised group I ever met, getting a bad time from the operation managers while trying to keep their workers motivated. They all had stress-related ailments, such as ulcers and cardiac problems, because they were under such immense pressure. Somebody had to keep the show on the road and they were the ones who did it. I had a really good relationship with them because I tried to make their jobs easier to do, which involved protecting them from the operations people. I got the supervisors to record stuff systematically and so our forced outage rate began to come down. I wanted these guys to have a nice job that they could do, instead of being constantly run off their feet, with a job being started and then fitters being transferred to do work elsewhere. I said that we weren't going to keep moving fitters around; when we finished one job, then we would start another. Helmut wasn't strong enough to be able to deal with the operations type of managers who were saying, 'We have to have this', and 'We have to have that'. These supervisors worked their asses off and were the only people there, as far as I was concerned, who justified their wages. It was a hugely unionised place, and if the boss doesn't have the right attitude towards work, it is very, very hard for anybody under them to lead because workers just say, 'Look at him … '.

I began to study maintenance engineering there and, for the first time, I found something in the company that really posed a challenge for me. I was solving problems in real time. This is where I came across the role of the subconscious – that was a huge discovery. In essence I learned not to try to analyse problems until the cows come home, but to walk away and wait for clarity to come.

I made the supervisors' lives easier for them. There was a so-called 'efficiency' meeting every week, which was essentially a 'beat up' session for the assistant maintenance engineer. Everybody started dumping on me and after a while I started fighting back. Eventually the operations superintendent said, 'You don't have to come to this. I will give you the list and you can prioritise. Keeping the plant on load and making the electricity is more important than the actual efficiency – if you can improve the efficiency, great, but continue making the electricity.'

Costs are fairly well controlled after you build a power station; you can shift them marginally but not dramatically.

We had problems with the condenser tubes; water was pumped in from the Liffey into a big condenser, which turned the steam back into water, which was then pumped back into the boiler. Mussels grew in the culverts carrying water to the condensers, so you would be digging tons of mussel shells out of a culvert when you took it out for maintenance. We used to inject chlorine into the water to try to kill the mussels, but it didn't work. A shell would get lodged in a tube and, with less space to pass through, the water would accelerate. There's an inverse relationship between speed and pressure, so the pressure dropped as the speed of the water went up; it dropped so much that the water would begin to boil at 10°C. A bubble of steam forms, pressure recovers as you go down the tube, the bubble of steam implodes and reforms as water. When that sort of implosion goes on for a while it cuts a hole in the tube, so salt water was going into condensed steam. That section of the plant would have to be shut down. A turbine is very precious and can take only very clean steam; a boiler can take only very clean water.

Chemists work on taking the town water, passing it through filters and chemicals to take particles out of it, and eventually processing it through polishers to ensure the steam will be clean enough.

I got a primitive maintenance system going there, which was really just a reactive system, recording what had been done, and the supervisors implemented it. I couldn't compensate for a very bad station manager, but there was some order in the system when I left that job.

After I left Ringsend, a member of the turbine cleaning team, 32-year-old Thomas Collier from Coolock, had to get into the condenser and block up a hole in the tube one day in August 1980. He was accidentally locked into the condenser; the water was switched on and he was killed. Disaster. That's what can happen without leadership.

My next post was in Bellacorick in County Mayo, where I went in 1979 to be assistant station manager. Commissioned in 1962, the Bellacorick station ran on milled peat and had a capacity of just 40MW.[4] I wasn't there two months when the Ringsend boss rang me and asked would I come back. This was because I had been running the place, not him. He was a guy I didn't like. I remember I had asked for a day's leave when Hildegarde's mother was dying and I needed to get back to Sligo, and he was quite reluctant to give it to me. I owed him absolutely nothing if that was his attitude.

I was in Bellacorick for less than two years. It was a lovely place to work and my expertise in maintenance came together there. I developed a maintenance system that was staggeringly excellent, although I say so myself. I was eventually able to summarise it on one page. I went through every unit of the plant and considered the consequences of each breaking down in terms of, cost, safety and knock-on effects. Some had scary consequences, such as the failure of an end bell on the turbine; if any water comes into contact with the end bell, a crack forms and it will run to breakdown in

4   Esbarchives.ie

24 hours. The turbine has to be designed so that no water can ever get in contact with the end bell. The system I designed concluded with a maintenance policy for every component. A whole range of policies can be applied, including condition monitoring and design out maintenance to running to breakdown, which included time-based inspections, use of new materials etc. There were also various kinds of condition-based maintenance, such as looking at the vibrations of a bearing or looking at the temperature of oil cooling.

The staff responded to leadership and, using my system, we brought failure levels right down to that of hydro stations. News of my success in doing so began to reach other parts of the organisation.

My nature is to strive to innovate, even in traditional areas that are not supposed to need any further innovation. This comes from something in my personality that doesn't want to accept the status quo.

I loved working in the maintenance area. Maintenance is about maximising the safety, availability, efficiency and financial returns from a bunch of assets that are already installed. It was the most exciting project that I accomplished while working in the ESB. Maintenance had been proving very difficult for the company at the time and I worked at it for roughly a decade, from 1975 to 1985. I found it satisfying because it was an area where real results could be accomplished. There are three pillars of maintenance management: analysing a difficult problem and proposing a solution; working with and directing staff to do the work; and instituting the method whereby the problem was solved by including it in a system, so that it is available to all future generations of managers, supervisors and craftsmen.

Fixing a plant-related problem is all about identifying what the problem is in the first place. Analysis is necessary, and here my engineering training was useful. I became familiar with a whole host of analytic equipment, ranging from X-rays, to dye penetrant, to endoscopy and ultrasonics. It was while doing this maintenance work that I was introduced to the properties of materials. The science of materials was then in its infancy, and it was exploding in range and scope, to the point today where planes are built from carbon fibre and glue, a combination that's stronger than aluminium and much lighter than steel.

The ESB was a very regimented company, with a deep divide between the engineering and administrative sides. Paddy Moriarty, who succeeded J. J. Kelly, an engineer, as CEO in 1981, came from an admin background, having been director of personnel. Accountants were in the admin line, and, when word got out about this plant maintenance model I had designed, they wanted to learn more. I was called in to a meeting with Bill Humphreys, regional engineering manager in charge of a cluster of power stations, and Kevin Kelly, the accountant on the admin side. Asked how much it would be to implement this maintenance strategy, I estimated £20,000; a lot of work had gone into it. Humphreys, who was not going to let me, a 32-year-old, determine how things should be run, said it was very expensive. However, Kelly told me to go ahead.

Humphreys walked out the door, saying, 'We'll have to think about that.' Kelly, following behind him, turned and simply said, 'Eddie, carry on … .' He was going to make it right with Humphreys.

Industrial relations were generally very good at Bellacorick. The main problem was staff who were alcoholics. There was nothing like the class differences at Ringsend, but personal antagonisms between people caused most of the difficulties.

A step up to section engineering manager in the ESB's generation department in 1981 sent me reluctantly into the maw of the beast, head office in Dublin. It was a promotion, as I was then running the overall maintenance programme for the whole country, trying to fit it into a window of opportunity in the summer, when demand for electricity was less.

A computer programme had been built by my predecessor over three or four years but it wasn't every efficient. I was called to a meeting where Chris Quinn, Deputy Head of the Generation Department, introduced me to a bunch of engineering inductees. I could choose one of them to come and work with me. I said, 'I want somebody who is shit hot at computers.' Martin McAdam, a fellow chemical engineer with a gigantic IQ, said, 'I'm your man.' Within six weeks he had written a great programme.

I set about visiting every station in turn to discuss their maintenance needs. I was changing things and telling people how they needed to change to become more efficient. I initiated a document that I called the Book of Estimates for the following year's overhaul programme. Although this was a huge improvement on what had gone before, it was not welcomed by the bosses in the department. All they wanted to know was the cost. Looking back I can see I didn't spend enough time selling the idea to my superiors. There was a lot of pressure in this job; mainly because I had to try and manage a host of specialist engineers who acted like consultant surgeons, and were very precious about having suggestions made to them by a much younger guy. The first person to blame when there was a shortage of plant was the guy doing my job.

A job came up for a PR officer in the ESB and I decided I would apply for that. I was ambitious and I am naturally a PR type of guy. I thought I might be given a chance. I got an interview for the post, for which Paddy Moriarty was doing the interviewing. Paddy would have heard about me at that stage and about what I had done at Bellacorick, because the ESB was like a family, really.

At a certain stage in the interview Paddy said, 'What age are you, Eddie?'

'I'm 35.'

'Could it be said you are a bit young for the job?'

To which I replied, 'Nobody asked Napoleon what age he was at Austerlitz.'

Paddy nearly fell off his chair. That is exactly the kind of thing he appreciated. After the interview, as I made my way back to the Generation Department, Chris Quinn came out of his office as I was going by and asked me, 'Did you really say to Moriarty that "nobody asked Napoleon what age he was at Austerlitz"?'

I didn't get the job because Paddy wasn't looking for an Eddie O'Connor; he wanted somebody who would be his master's voice and he knew I wasn't going to be that.

At the beginning of 1984, I was sent down to be maintenance manager at the coal-powered station of Moneypoint in County Clare. I wanted to do the planning job there, but I was told I had to do line management. Pat O'Brien was station manager and I got on very well with him. However, when I proposed that the payroll department switch from using a system of cash in brown envelopes to money going straight into workers' bank accounts, he said I would never get the workers to agree to it. There was still a tradition among men of not wanting their wives to know exactly what they were earning. They would just hand over 'housekeeping' money and keep the rest for themselves.

However, in the 1980s, when sectarian violence was rampant in Northern Ireland, armed robberies were a regular occurrence in the Republic. At the time, workers all over the country were being paid weekly wages in brown envelopes and the transit of all this cash created easy targets for criminals. I called in the shop stewards and explained that in the light of all the armed robberies it wasn't a good idea for a van to be calling to the plant with wages for 300 to 400 people. I pointed out that transporting money in that way was getting increasingly dangerous and people were getting shot.

'If the van gets hit, you won't get paid,' I remarked. The shop stewards saw the point and said they agreed to the switch.

When I went back to Pat to tell him the lads had agreed, he was astounded. To me it was just another bit of work: sit down and communicate with people to persuade them that something is the right thing to do. That's leadership. Present the problem and ask people how we're going to solve it.

I played rugby locally while I was at Moneypoint and I remember a red-haired Anthony Kelly being a most conscientious member of the team who never missed training. He went on to become a high-profile, convicted criminal in Limerick who survived various assassination attempts.

I expected to be working there about 10 years, having asked Pat soon after I arrived how long he anticipated I would be there. After renting for a while, Hildegarde and I bought a site and had a timber-framed house built on it in the nearby coastal town of Kilrush. However, I had only been in Moneypoint two years when, one day in December 1985, I was told one of the national directors, Alf Kelly, had arrived at the plant asking to see me. I thought I had been found out.

'There has been a job on the board for fuel-purchasing manager,' he said.

'I saw that,' I said, 'but I haven't applied.'

'We noticed that. Why not?'

'I didn't think that I would get it.'

'Well you could be wrong there.'

'Oh really?' I responded. I knew that was his way of saying the job was mine if I applied, so I did, naturally. When a director shows up and tells you should be applying for a really top job, which was at least three levels up from the grade I was on, you do it.

There was reorganisation going on at the time and that job had been vacated by John Lang, who was on that first interview panel when I joined the company, and was now a director.

I was interviewed the day before Christmas Eve 1985 and I think they had a special board meeting that day and appointed me.

Within a matter of weeks, I wasn't going to be living in County Clare with my wife and family but was going back to Dublin to be in charge of spending around £240 million a year.

Although we never got to live in our new house in Kilrush, Hildegarde was delighted to get back to Dublin with our two children, Lesley and Robert, who were very young at the time.

I showed them at the ESB that we were out of pocket, having been forced to put our house on the market so soon after construction and during recessionary times in Ireland, and I needed compensation if I were to take the job. They readily agreed to make up the difference between the price I got for the house and the building costs.

The first thing I had to do was reorganise the fuel-purchasing department at head office, but I reckoned I had enough staff as the work was all about negotiating contracts. The highlights during my one and a half years there included travelling to coal mines in Australia with Paddy Moriarty. I got to know him very well. He was a very wise man, very cool. Paddy was a big patriot. He refused to take up the additional payments that most CEOs would have had. Later on, when he had severe kidney damage as a result of taking beta blockers to control his blood pressure, he refused to be given a donor kidney. 'That should go to a younger person,' he said. He died from kidney failure at the age of 72.

Organising that Australian trip was one of the first tasks of my new secretary, Marian Shanahan, who had transferred to my office from another department in June 1986. Little did we know then that more than 34 years later she would still be making all my travel arrangements and appointments. She followed me into BNM and, while she stayed on there to work for my successor, Paddy Hughes, for a couple of years, I persuaded her to join me in my new company, Future Wind Partnership, towards the end of 1999.

During my time as fuel-purchasing manager, I signed a big contract with Bord Gáis – with my old friend Gerry Fahey, who was assistant chief executive there and who had done chemical engineering with me in UCD. I bought coal from Australia, Poland, the US and Colombia. I think we bought it through Shell who were based in Miami. Pittsburgh was also a place I went to quite a bit. I have always liked to travel.

You ate in the finest places when men came to town selling coal. Le Coq Hardi in Ballsbridge, a favourite haunt of the late controversial Taoiseach Charles Haughey, was the main place in Dublin at the time and expensive wine flowed freely. Purchasing was a very specific task, involving the negotiations of big contracts and making sure the coal was up to scratch. The ash fusion melting point was a big thing – if the ash fuses at too low a temperature it just sticks to the tubes and inhibits heat transfer. You had to be sure you were buying the right quantities. There are three types of 'tons': the old-fashioned, 2,240 pounds in a ton; then there's a 'tonne' – the metric ton, 2,200 pounds; and, finally, the US 'short ton', which is 2,000 pounds. You had to know what you were buying. I came across little elements of corruption here and there, not in the ESB, but in other foreign utilities.

We were into one bad contract that I tried to get out of but I couldn't. Despite trying every possible legal remedy I could not extract us.

I remember when a purchasing manager for one of the Danish utilities invited all the world's coal suppliers to celebrate a milestone birthday with him. It would be a mean man who wouldn't give him a decent present for a major birthday! I would never have anything to do with that sort of thing, and Hildegarde was always a big one for separating your job from your private life. I don't have that luxury but I do have a whole bunch of friends who have nothing to do with the job.

When I was down in Moneypoint I had become aware what an amazing port it is – just 30 metres from the shore you have 30 metres in depth. There isn't a ship in the world that has a draught of 30 metres, so you could bring in any ship of any size in the Shannon Estuary and offload it. They had these incredible offloaders that would grab tons of coal and deposit the load on a system of belts that would move it to be laid down in the coal yard. I nearly had a heart attack when I saw these stacker/reclaimer machines – I was supposed to be in charge of maintaining them, and I had no clue how they worked. They were all driven by a vast array of computers – in the days when you could still see your computers.

However, I had made my name as a maintenance engineer and I knew that there was no problem that can't be solved. I was very interested in transhipping coal through Moneypoint – you could have used ship unloaders there to put coal into smaller boats and transport them to other ports. There were two people in the company who believed that could work – me and Paddy Moriarty. I went off to Galway one morning to speak to the Irish Ports Association at a 10 o'clock meeting. 10.15 and 10.30 passed, and I was just getting up to leave when the secretary came out and said, more or less, 'Not everybody is pleased to see you; you can speak for 10 minutes and then you'll leave.'

I went in and told them it was a great opportunity for them, that we could import coal from anywhere in the world at Moneypoint, for an awful lot less than the individual ports could do themselves, and then redistribute it around the island.

The port owners were apoplectic with rage and fearful; they couldn't get their heads around the fact that I wasn't trying to compete with them for selling coal. I wanted to use Moneypoint as a transhipping centre, just like Rotterdam, which a lot of them were using for breaking bulk – the transfer of transcontinental loads into smaller vessels, to be transported to different destinations. The port owners wanted nothing to do with the proposals. In any case, the unions and management in Moneypoint and all the workers in the

ESB were not going to countenance me orchestrating this sort of diversification, so the whole thing came to nothing.

However, decades later, Moneypoint is back in my future thinking. The station is going to be closed in 2025. There is this enormously valuable asset, a big port with a significant lay-down area. I can see it would be extremely useful in my vision of getting Ireland generating 75,000MW of wind energy in the Atlantic and shipping it across the Supergrid into Europe as part of the overall decarbonisation solution.

I always like a challenge and, as a fuel-purchasing manager, once your contracts were established, it was more a matter of keeping things ticking over. After a year and a half, I applied for the managing director post at another semi-state company, BNM, which was responsible for developing the country's peatlands and supplying our turf-fired power stations. However, the ESB had been a great company to work for. I had all kinds of experiences there; they recognised talent and promoted it, but I was too ambitious and impatient to hang around.

CHAPTER 3

Arriving at Bord na Móna

F alling world oil prices during the mid-1980s were good for the ESB but not for BNM. Just before I arrived to work there, the price of world traded energy had fallen by 65%, due to a combination of a falling dollar and a falling price for crude oil, which had been at elevated levels since the two oil shocks of the 1970s.

BNM was and is a state-owned company. These companies were called semi-states at the time, because nominally independent boards were appointed to run them and they were supposed to be commercial entities. They dated from a time when entrepreneurship and the availability of investment capital in Ireland were limited. BNM was set up in 1946. This was just after the Second World War, during which the country had to rely on its own meagre energy resources. Peat was burned in homes and commercial buildings, and a major proportion of electricity was generated by burning sod and milled peat.

BNM had three different products, all based on harvested peat. The bulk of the operation was associated with manufacturing five million tonnes of milled peat for sale to the ESB. There were four briquette factories manufacturing a solid brick of dried peat for use in homes and factories. There was a horticultural product, which was an excellent growing medium for plants.

At the same time, the government's benevolent attitude to state enterprises was changing and the cold wind of commercial reality started to blow through once comfortable corridors of complacency. Huge debt, industrial relations problems and government demands for cost-cutting hung over BNM, and two successive bad harvesting seasons in 1985 and 1986 heightened the sense of crisis over its future viability.[5]

That was what I walked into in July 1987 when I became the first managing director at BNM to be appointed from outside the company since its inception in June 1946. Systematic draining of Ireland's bogs and harvesting of peat began in the 1930s, primarily as a way of providing jobs for people living in the Midlands, where there was little other economic activity. A former ESB man, C. S. ('Todd') Andrews, who had joined the Department of Industry and Commerce in 1933, set up the Turf Development Board as a state-owned company financed by the exchequer to coordinate the peatland work schemes. Until my arrival as CEO, the company had been funded by government-guaranteed debt. This stood at close to £200m at the time of my appointment.

More than 50 years after its foundation, when BNM was looking for somebody to lead a total overhaul of the company, I fancied the challenge. The chairman, Brendan Halligan, who was to become a close friend, recalled having had a 'gut feeling' that I was the right man for the job the moment I entered the interview room during the recruitment process and before he knew anything about me. I had to walk quite a distance from the door to a chair that was facing a table, behind which he was chairing the interview panel.

'There was a swagger about him and an air of self-confidence,' Brendan said of me later. He had always liked leaders, be it in politics, business or whatever field. That day he was unaware that our paths had crossed before, 18 years earlier, during the 1969 general election campaign when Brendan was General Secretary of the Labour Party.

5   Donal Clarke, *Brown Gold: A History of Bord na Móna and the Irish Peat Industry*, Dublin: Gill Books, 2010.

He had appointed a mutual friend, Niall Greene, as campaign director for Connacht-Ulster. Niall didn't drive so I drove him and his wife Nuala around in a rented Mini. I was never a formal member of the Labour Party but they would have been closer to my political convictions at the time than any other party. I met all the Labour candidates running in the Connacht-Ulster region in that election, including a future President of Ireland, Michael D. Higgins, who didn't win a seat that time in the Galway West constituency, nor at his next attempt in 1973, but did go on to have a highly successful political career, being elected TD in 1981 for the first time.

The BNM interview panel shared Brendan's view on my suitability for the top job and the board unanimously recommended me as first choice of three names submitted to Minister for Energy Ray Burke, who was keeping a close eye on the recruitment process. He called me in for a personal 10-minute interview before the government formally ratified the appointment, during which he gave me a very clear brief 'to get the f***ing place organised'. The salary scale and other conditions of appointment were outlined in a letter of 15 July 1987. As the salary was below the maximum level and 10% below what I was earning in the ESB, Brendan made representations on behalf of the board and succeeded in getting a new letter of appointment issued on 20 July, allowing the board discretion to fix the remuneration within a specified range. It decided to fix the annual salary at the top end of the scale.

The board was very conscious that I was being offered a post where the risks were high, the chances of success questionable and that I would be leaving an apparently secure and attractive future in the ESB. I was being asked to turn a loss-making, moribund organisation into a dynamic, commercial enterprise. They agreed that the chairman should work out with me what resources I needed to do my job as managing director and that the details should remain confidential between the two of us.

Before my appointment, Brendan had gone to my boss, ESB chief executive Paddy Moriarty, to tell him what was intended. His response was more or less 'damn you', that he had seen me as his successor in years to come, but he said he wouldn't stand in the way of BNM appointing me. He gave Brendan his blessing for this poaching by one semi-state company from another.

Almost the entire focus of BNM then was on its production of peat from the boglands. It sold around five million tonnes of milled peat a year to the ESB, which at that time enjoyed a monopoly to supply the country with electricity. As its major customer was compelled to buy its biggest product, it is not surprising that BNM operated without the basic commercial concepts that are essential for survival of any company in the private sector. Things like the need for profitability, customer appreciation, productivity, long-term strategy, product development, integrated machine design and construction, and even debt management, were not generally accepted as core to the company. My job was to change all this. When I joined, the company had sales of £100 million, debts of £200 million and losses of £17.5 million. There had been 19 strikes in the previous 20 months. I really had no idea what the underlying problems amounted to.

I suspected I would be required to play the classic role of a change agent. The words of Machiavelli in *The Prince* come to mind: 'The leaders who would change the present order will have all those who benefit from the current order as enemies, and but lukewarm support from the ones who will gain from the change.'

I commissioned a comparative study between BNM and Finnish peat company VAPO. BNM's productivity had been lagging far behind that of the Finns – 1988 figures showed that while we produced 1,700 tonnes of peat per man per year, they were producing 3,400 tonnes. What was just as damning was the fact that BNM productivity had been static for 20 years.

I decided to meet with each production centre, asking the shop stewards and any other natural leaders to attend each meeting with me. There could have been 20 to 40 people in the room, and each was invited to speak about the problems they saw in the company. Most of the staff I met had never seen the managing director before.

They were clear and emphatic in their judgements about what was wrong. The staff are the people who are most critical of a company because they see the problems at first hand. They discuss them with each other and feel the consequences because they affect their day-to-day working lives and their futures.

There was a massive gap between head office and the production sites. Head office engineering came in for criticism. According to the staff, a design would arrive down from Dublin to the works to be constructed there. The fitter charged with building the machine would realise that, given the proposed design, it couldn't work and would sink in the bog. He would change it to make it capable of driving across the bogs. The engineer would arrive on site and realise his design was changed. Strong words would be exchanged. The engineer would go back to head office and issue a new drawing incorporating the local changes, without acknowledging the fitter who had made the difference. This angered the local staff more than any other issue. I determined at this time that the gap between the production units and head office had to be shortened physically as well as politically. The engineers would also have to change their ways.

At these meetings the staff did not point out that there were too many of themselves.

This set of meetings set the tone for my entire time in BNM. There were no more strikes, apart from an unofficial short stoppage in Shannonbridge when we introduced the Employee Enterprise Scheme (see page 40). Having met with 24 groups, I had a good outline of what was needed to run the company. To transform a company, a few external expectations have to be in alignment with the personal attributes of the person charged with leading the change. There has to be unity between board and management.

One of the more interesting aspects of the job was BNM's connection with the USSR. Only the USSR, Finland and Ireland harvested peat for energy. Soon after the October Revolution in 1917 Lenin established the peat industry. When Todd Andrews was setting up BNM he naturally went to Russia to learn how things were done there. There were protests in the 1950s when it emerged that the atheistic communist Russians had connections with a native Irish company. The Legion of Mary was prominent in the opposition to the BNM connection with the Russians. One of the stories with which I was regaled when I was just a few months in the job was the attitude of a former MD of BNM. He would alight from the plane in Sheremetyevo airport in Moscow and kiss the ground, announcing that he had arrived in paradise on earth.

My experiences with the Russians were altogether different.

The rouble had an official exchange rate with sterling. One pound got you one rouble, and you had to join a long official queue and sign multiple forms to make the exchange. Out on the street, teenagers were offering 15 roubles for a pound. This happened on the Monday I arrived in 1998. By that Friday the kids were offering 45 roubles per pound. Ordinary household commodities were very difficult to obtain there, and normal shopping had broken down as far as ordinary domestic consumables were concerned. It was not uncommon to see queues maybe 750 metres long waiting to buy peaches from the Black Sea area. People were paying a month's salary for a kilo of peaches.

Notwithstanding the money situation we were always treated like royalty when we arrived for official meetings. We used to meet with a 'minister', actually a civil servant, who had a mouth full of gold teeth. I recall he had about 12 phones on his desk, all different colours. If one worked that would be the height of it. We would meet at around

10 am and the first thing we usually did was sign a memorandum of understanding between both companies. We had to toast the newly signed cooperation agreement. Following a tray of 10 beers, we were stuck into the vodka from 10.30, which I had the strong impression was the point of the exercise.

At gatherings of the international peat society, the various participants would inform each other about the production in their home countries. The Russians talked about the Five-Year Plan calling for 100 million tonnes to be produced each year. When we last met in 1991 (after Glasnost and Perestroika) in Amsterdam the Russian minister announced that a million tonnes had been produced that year. Basically, he hadn't a clue what was happening in the country during the communist regime. It was the final confirmation for me that this political system had completely failed.

Brendan Halligan was a great chairman. He recognised that a tough transformational job had to be done and realised nobody was going to like it. He saw his role as being supportive of myself and senior management staff rather than trying to second-guess us. That gave us the freedom to be entrepreneurial on day-to-day business. The conversations would be all about change and future possibilities.

Brendan would also encourage people to get to know each other socially, beyond the confines of the boardroom and the office. Sometimes he and the non-executive directors would go to the pub after board meetings.

While Brendan and I worked very well together, he was strongly opposed to my idea of moving our head office from Baggot Street to Newbridge, County Kildare. I became convinced that the official BNM headquarters would be better off closer to the production works, and that the company should move to Newbridge. We were housed in a very stylish, iconic building, designed by eminent Irish architect Sam Stephenson and situated right in the middle of the government quarter of the city. He believed it made a statement about the prestige of the company. From the public affairs point of view, he was adamant that BNM HQ should stay in the middle of the action rather than relocate to what he regarded as little more than 'a few sheds' down the country.

However, I believed not only that it made financial sense if this valuable Dublin property could be leased or sold to reduce our debt, but moving to the site of our expanding R&D operations would bring improved synergy. We would also be closer to our production heartlands, something that would be appreciated by the production staff, and would bring the designers and manufacturers closer together physically. There was a building earmarked as suitable for refurbishment as offices at Newbridge, where an experimental station was first constructed in 1946. I convinced the worker-directors that we would be much better off on one campus and they worked on Brendan. He finally gave in, saying he wasn't going to try to stand in our way, but he made clear that he still regarded it as a 'bloody awkward and most inconvenient' move that was being made against his will.

The board made the formal decision to relocate the head office in early 1993, by a vote of nine to two. It also required legislative change, as there had been a statutory requirement that the head office be 'in the City of Dublin'.[6]

When we were planning the move to Newbridge I had asked to meet all the staff who were working in our head office. I particularly remember my visit to the 'printing unit'. Its function was a necessity, I was told, because 'we still have a lot of forms'. It wasn't clear if there was anybody in charge but there were four guys working in this room in the middle of the building, where there were rows and rows of pigeonholes containing a fine array of forms, including some written in the old Irish script, Cló Gaelach, that had been phased out in the 1950s. Most of the forms were piled in the

---

6   Donal Clark, op. cit.

pigeonholes, covered in a thick layer of dust. These guys did absolutely nothing; this was one of the easier sections to close down because nothing was happening there.

When we were just about to move to Newbridge, I called all the head office staff to a meeting in the boardroom. I explained that we were going to relocate the entire head office, refurbish the building, and then lease or sell it. I delivered these messages in the clearest possible terms. I recall one of the staff saying, 'You are a terrible manager because you never tell us the truth.' It brought to mind the words of Mao Zedong, that one finds what one brings. This particular person didn't want to hear that his job was moving, so despite my having said it clearly at least three times he never heard it.

I set up an internal task force of four guys led by Paddy Hughes, who was one of the more successful managers there before I came in, to look at what needed to change. A straight, highly intelligent man, Hughes was somebody everybody respected. I knew that if he became convinced of the need for reorganisation he would be able to bring everybody with him. When the task force duly issued a report that suggested the company be reorganised, this message to staff was coming from long-standing colleagues rather than a newly appointed outsider. The report recommended that the company be divided into three separate business units: one selling milled peat to the ESB for generating electricity; the second to be a solid fuels division to sell briquettes; and a third to look after sales of horticultural peat. This paved the way for radical change.

Everybody knew that having a workforce of 4,200 wasn't sustainable. I remember going on a training programme at the Irish Management Institute where I was intellectualising at a great rate about what was happening in BNM.

The guy giving the course said, 'Eddie, you know what's wrong with Bord na Móna. There are far too many people employed.'

Fair enough. I knew getting the staff numbers right was a crucial issue.

We introduced a redundancy programme. To do it without rancour or strikes was the challenge. I set about it according to the philosophy that you have to take people down to the gutter of despair first and remove all hope: I told the staff and their unions, 'The company is totally disorganised and the government is refusing to give us more money if we continue in this way.' Once the workers accepted that reality, which they knew better than me was the case, they would be delighted to get some money because next year there might be no money. Those leaving the company could take a redundancy payment calculated on the basis of four weeks' pay for every year of service, up to a maximum of 119 weeks. The government had to increase our debt slightly, but shedding 57% of the staff paid for itself very quickly. It was the most effective way to turn the company around.

It was commonplace in BNM for local public representatives to put pressure on local and head office management to hire people to the staff. In almost every case they were not needed. It gave me an insight into the democratic process.

Take, for instance, the closure of the briquette factory in Lullymore, County Kildare, in 1992. Kyran Hurley, a very brilliant manager whom I had recruited from outside the company in 1990 to head the solid fuels division, had come up with a plan that included the closing of one of our four briquette factories to address the problem of over-capacity. The board agreed it had to be done and Brendan briefed each of the relevant politicians privately before the decision became public knowledge through the media. He said the reaction was pretty much the same from all of them, along the lines of: 'I understand what you have to do and why you have to do it, but you will understand that I am going to have to criticise you in public.'

After the government and civil servants were made aware of our intention to shut down the Lullymore plant, it wasn't long before we were summoned to Leinster House to meet all the political representatives of County Kildare, including former Fine Gael leader Alan Dukes, his party colleague Bernard Durkan, Sean Power of Fianna Fáil and Emmet Stagg of Labour. I decided I was going to go in by myself, as it's much more difficult for a group to beat up on one guy. If I had brought in back-up, we would all have had a big row. The public representatives told me we couldn't close a factory, while I countered that while the government was refusing to give us any money, we had no choice but to close a loss-making operation. Dukes, as co-author of that government strategy (he was leader of Fine Gael when that party, out of government, had gone along with the Fianna Fáil government by promulgating the Tallaght strategy), never said a word during the meeting but, as a public representative, he couldn't not be there. I was also clear that even if we got state money, I would not advise that it be invested here as it was a very old plant, dating back to 1936, and past its time. It was costing us £1 million a year to operate, and demand for the product, peat briquettes, was falling. Yet still the politicians wanted a compromise; to kick the can down the road and keep it open for another year.

'But I don't have another million, so we really have to close it now,' I responded. 'The workers will get a severance package and, as the country is on the up, they should not be unemployed for too long.'

'What are we doing listening to this man? This is all rubbish, I am going to the Civil Service to get this closure stopped,' declared Stagg as he left the room.

It was all a matter of going through the motions. The politicians could say to their constituents that they brought in the BNM managing director and gave him a hard time, and he told us the government wouldn't give BNM any more money. They become your defenders if you handle it properly.

We closed the plant.

As well as the redundancy programme, proposals for a pioneering Employee Enterprise Scheme were presented to staff. The idea stemmed from my deputy, Sean Grogan, who told me about how his father used to say to him that if you want a top outcome you should pay by results. The plan initially was that people who left the company could form multi-disciplinary teams who would then lease bogland from the company and the machinery needed to harvest the peat on it.

We will pay you per tonne of peat you produce, we told them, not by the hour – as that was what was killing the place. Many of those working on the bogs had got time-wasting down to a fine art, particularly on a fine summer's day, so they could stay on for overtime. Much of the activity of the staff was aimed at creating overtime for themselves. When the sun shines, it is imperative in peat-harvesting to make the most of every minute because it could be raining tomorrow – and it usually is.

I recall one of the gripes of the production staff at the time was the way management didn't allow them to take a tea break when they were out working on the bogs. Bogs are huge open areas. Workers could be working anywhere. Tea centres were local and the staff had to drive to them for their tea break. It could take up to half an hour to drive to a tea centre, so a nominal tea break of 10 minutes could involve not working for over an hour.

Sean Grogan and I had a close relationship, and he was an excellent manager. One day we were discussing how we could organise the workforce, given that there were now far fewer of them. He recalled how his father had always extolled the virtues of payment by results. What would happen if we paid each member of staff per tonne of quality product?

Thus we proposed the Employee Enterprise Scheme. We offered ex-employees a scheme whereby they were put together in small teams of four, including driver, production workers and a fitter.

They would be given a new set of equipment, control over a certain area of bog and would be paid per tonne of quality product. We trained them in team management and the new methods we were suggesting they use. I recall going down to the centre where five teams were being trained. I explained that, among other things, they should be aware that they were now taking weather risk. They asked what I meant by that remark. I reminded them that in 1985 a mere 30% of the production target was realised, on account of bad weather. They laughed and told me, 'That'll never happen, boss'.

These five little teams that were set up for the production season of 1989. As the old adage suggests, 'the Lord helps those who help themselves'. We had unbroken great weather for the entire summer and the teams made out like bandits. Tea breaks were taken on the hoof. There was no upper limit to what the company would pay and the teams, quite rightly, were rewarded for their courage in taking on a new system. The rest of the production staff could see what was happening, so there were demands that the scheme be extended to the rest of the company. It became a demand of the unions that all staff be allowed to work in small, demarcation-free teams. Thus the production issue in the company was solved.

When planning the Employee Enterprise Scheme we ran a conference in the Montague Hotel near Portlaoise for staff and members of the public. We brought in some eminent speakers, including Charles Handy, one of the management gurus of the time. I had been trying to popularise the idea of entrepreneurship. The conference was a success in the sense that it led to a wider political debate on the changes we were making in BNM.

Both the political left and the right were in agreement with the changes we were proposing for the company. The Workers' Party concluded that their belief in state enterprises compelled them to support someone who had a plan to make them work. The right, represented by the Progressive Democrats, believed in individual enterprise, and saw what was happening in BNM as a worthwhile example of that. Fianna Fáil was in power at the time, and they led in their customary manner, which was generally supportive of the semi-state companies they set up. Fine Gael made no comment one way or the other. The Labour Party, the most conservative party, were heard to mutter old slogans such as 'No contractors here'.

To the trade unions who protested, saying they believed in employment, my answer was: 'You can have your principles or you can have a company but you can't have both. Which do you want?' I believe the way to deal with people is face to face and you tell them the truth. People can accept things, however bad they may be, if they are told the truth.

Team members were reliant on each other to maximise their output and earnings, which eliminated the demarcation issues that had dogged the company. It meant that the fitter, who was responsible for maintaining the machinery, would also make peat when he had no maintenance to do. Through this approach we aligned what the workers wanted – more money – with what the company needed – lots of cheap, good-quality peat. This was a phenomenal innovation. It changed the rules of engagement and everybody was a massive winner.

The redundancy programme had to be carried out before we could introduce the Employee Enterprise Scheme. We introduced it during a general election. A young politician, Brian Cowen, was seeking to get elected for the first time. His home constituency was Offaly, which was the heartland of BNM. He was put under pressure by the unofficial strikers at Shannonbridge, and he complained about my changes to the Minister of Energy, Michael Smith. I was called in to a meeting with Michael. It was, from my viewpoint, a seminal meeting. It was quick. He asked me what was happening in Shannonbridge. I told him about the unofficial action (which he knew already). He asked me what could happen next. I told him the action could spread to the whole of Shannonbridge. He then asked what could happen after that. I told him that I thought nothing else would happen, but in a worst-case scenario, it could spread to other works. I told him about the way we had prepared the workforce for the changes, with extensive communications with shop stewards and unions. He asked me what was the worst thing that could happen. I said, 'Well, I suppose the whole company could go on strike.' To which he replied, 'Thank you.' I could see the meeting was at an end, so I thanked him and got up to leave. As I neared the door of his office he said, 'Don't stop, Eddie, keep going.'

The meeting would have allowed him to say to Brian Cowen, 'I called in the MD and I had strong words with him.' I speculated that he told Brian not to worry, and not to amplify what could have become a difficult situation.

The redundancy scheme cut employee numbers from 4,200 to 1,800 over three years. Then, with the enterprise scheme in place, output per head increased from its 1989 level of 1,750 tonnes per annum to 5,400 tonnes by 1995.

The unions could see it was the way to turn around the company and I didn't have a single official strike over the changes. Rather, the workers took ownership of it. That was my job as managing director, to help the staff save BNM. It was a beautiful arrangement because the redundancy programme, the divisionalisation and the Employee Enterprise Scheme looked after the bread and butter and turned BNM into a profitable company.

There is perhaps no more succinct comment on the new corporate culture that was being fostered within the company than that made by one of the worker-directors, Lal Daly.

'This is working,' proclaimed Lal. 'A man was seen yesterday running across the Boora Bog … .'

On the ground, we introduced a new system of peat production, the Haku system, copied from Finland. The garnering of peat in stockpiles of up to 100 tonnes, rather than in the traditional long narrow piles called reeks, was more efficient for various operational reasons, not least because the peat was better protected from the elements. The reeks had a much bigger surface area, which got wet faster. The Haku system led to a lower moisture content in the peat.

Another change, again borrowed from Finland, was a new way of making electricity from peat, using fluidised bed boilers. It's very hard to grind peat for burning. Coal can be milled to the consistency of very fine talcum powder, because it is a brittle material. This gives a huge surface area that allows oxygen to get to carbon which, at the right temperature, will burn. It's easy to burn the coal almost completely, so that the smoke stacks in modern power stations will be 'clean', with very little particulate carbon left in them. Although peat is also milled, it will never become as fine as coal and, as a result, there's always a lot of unburnt residue going up the stack.

I remember going to the US to have a look at fluidised bed boilers there. They require the suspension of a bed of peat in very hot sand with air blowing in at the bottom. It doesn't have to be milled and it remains in the bed until it has all been burned. Lullymore had a fluidised bed boiler installed and it worked very well.

One of the biggest issues to be addressed during my tenure at BNM was the dilapidated condition of the peat-fired power stations. They were 20 to 30 years old at the time. While it was no one's fault, they were dirty. Finely divided peat leaks out through any small cracks or holes and it gets everywhere. I was determined to change all the power stations to a new method of burning peat using fluidised bed technology.

We got £25 million from Europe to switch to this system, for what I called the new Europeat power station, now called Edenderry. This was an extraordinary achievement, which surprised even me, because there was a lot of opposition in Europe to the harvesting of peatlands. The more advanced elements in Europe understood before I did that one of the best ways of mopping up carbon was with bogs; they are more efficient than trees at absorbing carbon. By the time I got into BNM the bogs were drained and dead, so they were no longer functioning carbon sinks. A native bog is 95% water – there's more solids in milk than in bog. However, if you put in drainage channels, the water flows off and, when the weather gets fine, you can mill the surface, harrow the resulting crumb to turn it and dry it, until you have a substance suitable for burning.

Some of the sidelines we were developing were more about symbolism and creating a new image of the company. I was very taken with a piece of bog oak wood that was presented to me after speaking at a conference. Oak wood is a by-product of bogs, which kill everything in their path. They flood the trees, which, starved of oxygen, can no longer grow and collapse into the bog. A hard wood like oak is preserved in the bog. You can take this wood that has been in the bog for thousands of years and polish it and it makes a very fine ornament. Artist Michael Casey sculpted this wood at his workshop and studio beside Lough Ree at Barley Harbour in Newtowncashel, County Longford. I suggested we form a joint venture with Michael, providing him with his raw material for free. Helen Conneely came on board to do the marketing for the new company, Celtic Roots. After I left BNM they offered me the chairmanship of it. However, I felt they really didn't want to be burdened with a *persona non grata* in the eyes of the BNM chairman, so I declined.

We also set up the Clonmacnoise and West Offaly Railway in 1992, on which visitors could make a nine-kilometre trip to the Blackwater Bog. A venture like this wasn't about making profits, although it did wash its face financially, but rather to popularise the bogs and educate people about what we were doing. It was also a tourist asset in the Midlands, which didn't have many visitor attractions at the time.

The state is the nominal owner of BNM. In effect this meant strong oversight by the Civil Service. They controlled the company by having someone on the board. Being non-commercial, their overall goal was to prevent risk-taking by the company.

With a chairman like Halligan, relations with the Civil Service were kept at a good working level. This all changed when a new chairman was appointed. However, relations with the Civil Service were not all downside for me.

A most important contribution to my working and personal life was made by Eoin O'Neill, the departmental appointee on the board. In 1989 he told me about the role of CO_2 and other greenhouse gases that were causing heating of the atmosphere. Initially I was astounded to hear this. Almost all electricity at that time, and indeed still, is made by burning fossil fuels; coal, gas and oil. I remember rejecting the concept, and arguing that CO_2 was breathed out by all animals, so how could such a natural product be harming the biosphere? Eoin urged me to read up on the work of John Tyndall, a renowned scientist from County Carlow. While working at the Royal Institution in London in 1861, Tyndall passed radiation through various gases and observed what happened. Oxygen and nitrogen, the two main constituents of air (amounting to more than 99%) were observed to allow the radiation to pass through them with no effect. CO_2, on the other hand, absorbed the radiation, causing heat.

It was one thing to reject a concept emotionally because it posed all kinds of moral and practical dilemmas. It was another thing altogether to deny science. This intervention by Eoin O'Neill caused the greatest emotional, intellectual and commercial upset in my life. Here I was, the leading polluter in Ireland, responsible for organising the emission of more than 10 million tonnes of CO_2 per year. I slowly started to do something about it. I set up an Environmental Products Division and a small division whose goal was to build wind farms, headed by Paul Dowling. BNM participated in the building of Ireland's first commercial wind farm on our land, at Bellacorick in County Mayo. It is still running today, with its tiny 250kW turbines, taking free fuel from a windy environment and turning it into electricity.

The Environmental Products Division made use of the unique properties of the bog cotton roots, which extend down into the bog by up to a metre. They are of little use as a fuel, or as a horticultural product. They do, however, make an exceptional bio filter. There were two products, Puraflo and Biophore. Puraflo is used as a biodigester of the noxious water emanating from septic tanks. Septic tanks are used extensively in rural Ireland in houses that are not connected to a central sewage disposal system. Biophore bio-digests noxious fumes coming from chemical and pharmaceutical production plants.

Both products act as bio-filters. Bugs naturally evolve when presented with a food source. The organic chemicals coming from septic tanks and pharma plants act as feeds for the specialist bio-digesting microorganisms. The bugs grow naturally. Both products really work, and could, in time, have become the basis of taking BNM beyond peat.

It was only after I left BNM that I was able to make an onslaught on curbing CO_2 emissions.

CHAPTER 4

Entrepreneuring Bord na Móna

The reorganisation of BNM was the foundation for growth and diversification. In 1990, to set out my vision, I wrote an article, nominally for a 2010 edition of the *Chicago Tribune*. It featured a company, once a 'quintessential bog company in Ireland', expanding its operations in the US. The idea was to show how BNM was capable of transforming itself into a company with an international sales and product base. We reckoned we had only about 30 years' peat reserves left, so increased research and development was essential to pioneer new products. The use of peat in generating the country's electricity was steadily declining, from around 30% in the 1950s, to about 13% when I joined the company in 1987, and it was down to about 9% by the time I left.

I believed that over the next two decades, BNM could become a highly profitable, global company as it diversified and acquired other companies. Our acquisition in October 1988 of Pouget Solami, a French manufacturer of horticultural peat products, for £2.2 million was a start. Although it involved no government guarantees, the civil servants at that time were very uneasy about state companies buying companies abroad (I was later spoken of as a 'dangerous visionary').

Brendan saw us as part of a 'triangular relationship' with politicians and civil servants. Politicians tell civil servants what the policy is, but they in turn advise politicians what the policy should be. There was a complicated mix of to-ing and fro-ing, with civil servants telling us how things should be and us telling them how we saw it and what we were doing. Civil servants don't want an agency within the control of their department to make a mistake and cause public disquiet because they want to protect the minister from any political embarrassment.

John Loughrey became secretary of the Department of Energy in 1988 and was much more interfering than his predecessor Joe Holloway. Sean Ó Muirí, an assistant secretary, was responsible within that department for BNM and he served on the board between 1990 and 1995. Brendan knew that while Ó Muirí was there ostensibly as 'the Minister's man', his real responsibility was to report back to Loughrey. However, Brendan regarded Ó Muirí as a man of high culture and integrity, an old-styler who was very committed to the state and to BNM as a development corporation. He thought Ó Muirí handled his relationship with Loughrey well and was a good influence, because he could see that what was being done in the company was being done in the public interest.

My father had warned me about Loughrey when he was appointed. There wasn't much of a description of what I was to look out for, just 'Watch your back.'

There is a clear difference between business and political leadership. Political leadership was explained to me by a Fianna Fáil TD, Henry Abbott – 'We recognise where the people are at and we are a millimetre behind them.' Business has a singular focus. A business leader is not required to have a view on every event that happens. Your job is to set industrial goals, and to base a plan around them, to control according to these plans, to organise the staff so they have clear reporting lines and motivate them to achieve the goals. A business leader can be charismatic, but it is rare to find a political leader who leads from the front. The job is to not offend too many of the electorate, so you can get elected the next time. Business leaders have to act like conductors of the orchestra. They have the string section (the staff), the woodwind section (the shareholders), the brass section (the customers), the bass section (the suppliers) the percussion section (the business commentators). The job is to keep all these stakeholders reasonably happy, and not allow any one section to get out of step with the others. It is like juggling. All the balls have to be kept in the air, all the time.

In 1991, with all the changes we had introduced, we were headed for a profit of £5 million. This was great. However, there was a huge international currency crisis at the time. I recall that George Soros bet big against sterling, and won. Other currencies, such as the Swedish krona, went into freefall. The Irish government acted to protect the Irish currency by raising interest rates. One of my finance staff came into the office and explained how we had to roll over a £6.25-million loan. He said the interest rate was 105%. In a state of complete shock I said I would have to think about that before giving the go-ahead. I did my research into alternatives, which I'm sure the finance staff had already done, and found out that there was nothing to be done except take the bad medicine. I rang him in the afternoon and said go ahead. He told me that the offer was no longer available, and we would now have to pay 117% interest. High interest rates turned a £5 million profit into a £10 million loss.

This provided the impetus for me to carry out a plan to get the debt forgiven. My first port of call was the Civil Service. Loughrey explained that the government would never agree to this. What he was actually saying was that he did not agree with removing the debt burden. His official apologist within BNM was the financial controller, who explained that the high debt was like a huge snow covering on the roof. It prevented ambitious CEOs from engaging in any risk activity whatever. It excused any underperformance. Very little was visible except the interest payments on the debt.

When my approaches to the Civil Service failed I tried the direct approach to Minister for Finance Ruairí Quinn. I wrote him a letter explaining that no matter what was done by management, the company was at high risk of failure due to the historic debt burden. This approach was successful. The government took the BNM debt onto its own balance sheet. This was the last significant, and one of the important building blocks of an unencumbered future BNM.

I believe it helped convince Loughrey that I was a liability that had to be disposed of. He bided his time until a new chairman was appointed. When appointed Pat Dineen had one goal in mind. This goal, as he explained later on, was to do as he was instructed by the Civil Service, and get rid of me.

There followed nine months of struggle which, latterly, involved a board meeting every week. Despite Dineen having the full weight of the government behind him, and the fact that he released confidential internal documents to the media, the board never voted to dismiss me. At the end of the day, almost exactly nine years after having been appointed, I resigned with an enviable package. At age 49 I had a pension equating to 90% of the pension I would have had if I had stayed until I was 65. It was index-linked and paid by BNM. Whatever happened in the future, my wife and family would be able to get by.

A study was carried out by one of the big accounting firms and their conclusion was that I had made some £2,000 million for the government as a result of my actions while CEO.

At BNM I did the job that was in front of me. It was a vast learning experience and I was glad to be able to do it. Due to the behind-the-scenes work of the Department of Energy, another string was added to my bow – how to deal with a very strong bully.

There was an aspect of the work I did in BNM that receives little attention, a lot less than it deserves. I deliberately set about changing the culture of the company. It was a classical production-focused type of company when I arrived. Culture is the sum of the attitudes and values shared by the management and staff of a company. It manifests itself in the stories and legends that are told in the company, particularly about the founder. An amazing aspect of culture is that the staff and management are largely unaware of it. Culture represents the 'way we do things around here'. It is immediately apparent to an outsider who visits the company. On a more profound level, culture answers the questions: What is good? What is not good? Or: What is valued? What is not valued?

I wanted to create a customer-focused company. I was told when I went into BNM that it would take seven years to bring about meaningful change in any company culture. As I learned more about the art and science of being a CEO, I realised that just focusing on the customer, while valid in its own right, would not be sufficient to start a process of culture change. A slogan I used to describe my outlook on staff and industrial relations was the phrase 'turning the genius loose'. It was probably completely misunderstood and much fun was made of it by friend and foe alike. It was an attempt on my part to celebrate the quality that was spread, broadly, among the staff in the company. It was done out of respect for their collective and individual skill and dedication. I think that many of the staff knew what I had in mind.

Did I manage to change the culture? Certainly not to the extent that I had in mind. With significant opposition in the Civil Service and their acolytes in the management structure, I would describe my endeavours as a work in progress. I was able to build on these first attempts at culture shaping when I set up Airtricity in 1997.

CHAPTER 5

Bord na Móna Endgame

t's hard to imagine what it is like to be a marked man in the eyes of the state. When I started to be hounded out of BNM in 1996, I would have had some supporters in the 'Rainbow Coalition' government, but when somebody is being portrayed as a crook, everybody keeps their head down.

For 16 weeks there was a stand-off between the board and the government over my future, which was played out in the national media. Selective leaks to newspapers made it look as if I was enjoying the high life at taxpayers' expense. It was being alleged that my salary and other perks exceeded government guidelines.

My solicitor, John Lavery, had asked me directly at the outset: 'Have you done anything wrong?'

'No,' I assured him.

'Then don't worry about it.' He got Frank Sowman, a solicitor with William Fry, on the job. He was fantastic.

Reports of the company buying wine and a time-share in a villa in Portugal made for eye-catching headlines designed to stoke righteous indignation amongst the public. I never visited the time-share villa, which was used a few times a year to reward particularly hard-working members of senior management and their families. Nor did I ever get any wine as any form of perk. I had bought a case of 1989 Haut-Brion and was going to give a bottle each to the members of the board as a Christmas present. As a gift, the value didn't amount to more than £50 or £60 a head. When Pat Dineen heard about this he made a big deal about repossessing it and giving the money back to the company.

As the controversy rumbled on, I was being asked by journalists why I wasn't resigning.

'Why should I resign?' I said. 'I haven't done anything wrong. I have run this company with great success.'

The government couldn't persuade the board, which was split between political appointees and others, to get rid of me. The four worker-directors wouldn't vote against me because they knew that all along I had been working according to the deal made by Brendan Halligan when he recruited me.

I believe the seeds of the controversy were sown with the appointment of Brendan's successor some months after he had finished his 10-year stint as chairman in 1995. Corkman Pat Dineen, a former executive chairman of Irish Steel, was chosen as BNM's new non-executive chairman in September 1995 by Michael Lowry, the Fine Gael Minister for Transport, Energy and Communications in the coalition government of the time (1994–97), made up of Fine Gael, Labour and Democratic Left. Dineen was a friend of the Tánaiste, Labour leader Dick Spring.

When Lowry became Minister for Transport, Energy and Communications in 1994, he pursued a very populist line, suggesting that there was a cosy cartel among the semi-states and that we were in cahoots with one another to defraud the customer. I think all he wanted to do was make a name for himself and deflect attention from his personal affairs. Lowry's star was very high at that time and Dineen was a staunch supporter of Fine Gael. The semi-state companies had been a creation of Fianna Fáil and were not, I think, particularly liked by Fine Gael, probably seen as vehicles for jobs for the boys. Apart from the ESB and Aer Lingus, which had grown into really well-managed companies, most of the rest were in various states of appalling. The government's liquidation of Irish Shipping in 1984 had shocked many, not least the 300-plus workers, who no doubt thought they had jobs for life and had to fight for years for any redundancy payment. It was a stark warning of what could happen.

Lowry was first elected to the Dáil for the constituency of Tipperary North in 1987. It emerged years later that he had availed of a tax amnesty put in place in 1993 by Finance Minister Bertie Ahern. At the time, the amnesty was presented as a 'last chance' for tax cheats; those who had made false declarations were warned that they risked up to eight years in prison.[7] Lowry later told the Dáil that in the 1992/93 tax year he received £208,000 from Dunnes Stores, which was not declared for tax purposes.[8]

The civil servants knew there was no substance behind Lowry's crusade against the semi-states but they had to investigate. The guy who came down to see us said, 'I don't believe it any more than you do but I have to ask you all these questions.' He was really very friendly during a meeting with me for about an hour and that was that. It all went away for a while.

However, from the first board meeting that Pat Dineen chaired, he made his intentions obvious. It lasted only about 10 minutes; he was making it clear that he was the new man and that he was going to run the show his way. At that meeting he ordered £1 million to be cut off central office overheads.[9] I took his approach as a signal that he wanted to get rid of me. I had looked at this guy's behaviour when he was in charge of Irish Steel and I could see him coming. He had form for replacing chief executives. I wish I could say the animosity was one-sided and that I was the offended one, but I gave as good as I got.

7   Michael Brennan, *The Irish Independent*, 23 July 2013.
8   Colm Keena, *The Irish Times*, 23 March 2011.
9   *The Irish Independent*, 2 May 1996.

I had brought the details of my contract, as agreed with Brendan Halligan, to Dineen's attention after his appointment. He wasn't happy with it and said that he would work with the department to ensure that I was paid at least at the same level, albeit in a different form.

I don't think I had ever seen my long-term future at BNM, but I certainly wasn't going to get cashiered by somebody who knew nothing about the business and who, it seemed to me, was acting out of his own ego. I wasn't going to be accused of being corrupt in any way so I was prepared to fight for as long as it took to clear my name. All I did was implement the deal that Brendan had proposed when I went into the place in 1987.

When all this was being rehashed nine years later, Brendan said the board at the time was 'anxious to minimise the unattractiveness of the post for a young executive aged 38 with good career prospects'. The board gave him carte blanche to work out a package he deemed appropriate to enable me to do the job and said that the details would remain confidential between the two of us.

From then on, Brendan believed he was mandated by the board to do what he did and bound by that requirement of confidentiality. However, he did not believe that he was being asked, nor did he try to do something that would circumvent government guidelines. As a group, the non-executive directors were doing their best for BNM in the most trying of circumstances. They knew that if my appointment didn't work out, they were unlikely to get a second chance at rescuing the company.

Energy Minister Ray Burke must have known Brendan had done some deal, but it was a case of 'hear no evil, see no evil'. The chairman had been told by Joe Holloway, department secretary, to get a chief executive and to lead a revolution. In the light of a salary cap for CEOs of semi-state companies at the time, Brendan and the rest of the board knew other elements would have to be added to my remuneration, such as health insurance and a car with a driver. There was also £1,000 of business expenses a month that he told me did not have to be vouched – an instruction that was confirmed to John Hourican when he became chief financial officer in 1989.[10] However, in giving me this allowance, Brendan made it clear that I was expected to entertain, sometimes at home. He believed very strongly that Hildegarde, as a wife in the home, should feel part of the whole thing. He came from a culture where keeping the family of senior staff right was regarded as part of sensible management. That's why I was also given provision to bring Hildegarde with me on four overseas trips a year. They knew that I was facing a mammoth task to reorganise the company, which would involve long hours, stress and travel away from home, both around Ireland and abroad. As I was leaving a permanent, pensionable job with the ESB, the deal also included an insurance product, a Sun Life of Canada bond, not only against death but in the event that I wasn't reappointed. The chairman knew that it wasn't out of the question that BNM could meet the same fate as Irish Shipping. This bond was later to become the subject of disagreement, with one member of senior management contending that BNM, rather than me personally, should be the beneficiary.

Although the package was negotiated with the chairman, I presumed at the time that some other board members would have known of the details. For instance, Brendan worked closely with Eoin O'Neill, who was technical adviser to the Department of Energy and was first appointed to the board in 1985. In O'Neill's case, there was no discussion or prior briefing about the appointment. He got a telephone call just before 8.00 one morning from Tánaiste and Minister for Energy Dick Spring, who said simply: 'Congratulations, you're a member of the board of BNM and I just wanted to get you before you read about it in the newspapers this morning.' That was the way things were done then.

10   Donal Clarke, op. cit.

O'Neill was presumably put there to give the department the inside track on what was happening and report back to the assistant secretary who oversaw the BNM file. He said later that although he was supposed to go in to the assistant secretary 'and squeal to him if anything that would embarrass the minister was going to happen, I never discussed any Bord na Móna business with them and they never asked me'. He reckoned they knew his answer would be that they should write to the managing director if they were looking for information. And in fact, within a year of his appointment, O'Neill left the department to work on the setting up of an innovation centre in Trinity College Dublin. That moved him beyond the Civil Service remit for the remainder of his time as board member until 1990, after which I brought him into my mentoring group.

In April 1996 I was in Canada for the 40th birthday party of my good friend Rory Smith, when the *Sunday Tribune* ran a story by Stephen Collins on 21 April that BNM management were deeply split over an auditors' report that Dineen had commissioned on my remuneration package. It said the government was also concerned about the findings, which had not yet been presented to the board, and claimed that I had received £141,000 in expenses over three years, of which £39,000 were unvouched. Nobody asked me for a comment before the story was published.

That Sunday, together with chief operations officer Paddy Hughes and finance director John Hourican, I put out a statement rejecting any suggestion of a management split. I told Cliff Taylor, who ran a follow-up in the *Irish Times* the following day, that a Price Waterhouse review of my salary arrangements was 'absolutely routine', and explained that Dineen, who was unhappy with the way my package was administered in some respects, wanted to organise it differently and to have everything completely transparent.[11]

11   Cliff Taylor, *The Irish Times*, 22 April 1996.

In the same newspaper a few days later, Kevin Myers, who knew me from the days of UCD student politics, came out to bat for me, describing me as in his Irishman's Diary column as a 'good and honest friend'. 'The particular details of the financial transactions within BNM do not interest me,' he wrote, adding: 'I will tell you this: Eddie O'Connor is an honest man.'[12]

However, thanks to 'Peat Throat', as journalist Frank Fitzgibbon[13] characterised the source of the leaks, controversy was building. After the BNM board met for six hours on Monday, 29 April, breaking up just after midnight, Dineen told the media that a second report into my pay arrangements by Price Waterhouse had been requested by the Department of Transport, Energy and Communications. He also said then that Brendan Halligan had written to him, offering to cooperate fully. Yet it was nearly two months before the former chairman, who knew everything about how the arrangements for my personal remuneration and business expenses were set up, was invited by his successor to address a board meeting, which was held on 19 June.

The flawed Gleeson guidelines capping the pay of semi-state CEOs, under which Brendan had to operate, were being acknowledged by commentators as a factor in the situation in which we all found ourselves. Finance journalist Brendan Keenan pointed out that I, as a public servant heading BNM, could not earn more 'than the pinnacle of the public service, the Secretary of the Department of Finance'. This, he said, 'is a nonsense in the new age where State companies must compete commercially or die'.[14]

Not surprisingly, 'Peat Throat' was back at work to give journalists some prejudicial details from the second Price Waterhouse report on my pay arrangements. On 9 June 1996, two Sunday

---

12   *The Irish Times*, 27 April 1996.
13   *The Sunday Tribune*, 28 April 1996.
14   *The Irish Independent*, 2 May 1996.

newspapers reported that my pay and benefits over nine years were worked out as topping £1.9 million.

At that stage, I decided I had to make my first public statement since the affair started. I pointed out that these stories appeared to be based on a draft report by Price Waterhouse, which had been presented to the board and given to the Department of Transport and Communications, a report that was fundamentally flawed because it included my business expenses, the majority of which were of no benefit to me personally.

As the debacle went on, it became clear to me that some civil servants in the department were nevertheless envious of my arrangement, and of the fact that I had a driver. I suspect that some saw themselves as being equal, in terms of ranking and how much they should earn, to someone in charge of a semi-state company, yet they had no appreciation whatsoever for what I achieved at BNM.

The previous week it had become clear that Price Waterhouse intended to include all business expenses, rather than just evaluate the expenses that were part of the personal benefits deal I had agreed with Halligan. The only possible reason for lumping everything in together was to grossly exaggerate what I was supposed to have earned. My lawyers had advised Price Waterhouse that I would only agree to a report focused solely on my benefits going to the board, as per the terms of reference. Instead, somebody chose to use a draft report about something totally different from what Price Waterhouse had been engaged by the board to examine, in order to do maximum damage to me. This caused not only more distress for me and my family but also, I believed, further ridicule for BNM. It was the second time within six weeks that a supposedly confidential report had been leaked to the media in this manner.

As well as repeated mentions in the media reports of the buying of wine and the time-share, there were also references to my 'massive' pension entitlements'. Not only did I not have a 'massive' pension, the pension arrangements that had been agreed had not been honoured at that stage. I suggested that was a real scandal – that after 26 years' service to the state in the ESB and BNM, I still had not been granted my pension entitlements.

The public was being told I earned £2 million from BNM over nine years. If that had been true, there would have been grounds for me considering my position. The reality was that I did not even earn close to half that amount over that time. Nobody could honestly expect me to walk away from a job to which I had committed some of my most productive professional years, on the back of a dishonest and concerted attempt to ruin my reputation.

As I outlined in a letter to every board member the following week, I was able to identify one of the documents that had been reproduced to accompany the article in the *Sunday Independent*. It was a schedule of items that had been given to me for comment by Price Waterhouse on 4 June 1996. Before I enclosed a copy of it with a letter to the chairman, my secretary had noticed that under the column 'Paid Date' for the fifth item in the schedule, namely 'Guest Qarters [sic] Orlando', the date should have read 27 June 1994 and not 1995. She amended the figure 5 to 4 in her handwriting on the copy of the schedule to be sent to the chairman. It was this amended copy, which was not sent to anybody else, that was in the photograph with the article.

I told the board members that my solicitors had brought this matter to the attention of the chairman, who had replied that the documentation referred to had not been leaked to the media by him or anyone with his authority and he refuted any implication to the contrary. However, I added that information that my solicitors had specifically requested the chairman to provide had not been forthcoming and that inquiries were continuing.

Two months into the saga, on 19 June 1996, the day Brendan Halligan was finally to sit down with the board, the *Irish Times* ran an editorial headlined 'A Shameful Spectacle'. It described the events that had unfolded 'as one of the most tawdry games of politics ever conducted around the affairs of a semi-state company'. In perhaps a side-swipe at rival publications, the writer suggested that 'if past form is anything to go on, within a day or two there will be selective revelations designed further to portray the managing director in the worst possible light. It is a disgraceful way for the business of a great state enterprise to be conducted. It tarnishes those directly involved. It humiliates the employees of Bord na Móna, including Dr O'Connor. And it is an affront to the taxpayer whose earnings have built the company from its foundations.' It was pointed out that a clear word from Halligan at any point over the course of the affair could have put an end to the public spectacle. 'His silence remains one of the most puzzling aspects of all.' Halligan had offered as far back as April to explain himself to the board, but still hadn't had his offer taken up at this stage.

The editorial concluded that my departure from BNM appeared inevitable, and an early resolution of the situation would be in the best interests of the company. 'That it should come to this is regrettable. That it should be so drawn out and so contrived as a public spectacle is shameful.' In pointing out that it would be in Minister Lowry's own interests to bring it to a speedy conclusion, it added: 'It is surely remarkable that so many issues within Mr Lowry's purview seem to terminate in recrimination and grief.'[15]

Commentators were describing this as a political nightmare for Lowry, whose handling of semi-state issues was already suspect. With the board divided over what disciplinary action, if any, should be taken against me, it was increasingly looking like the buck was going to be passed to the minister. Only he could authorise my removal from the job, since I was employed directly by the department, but, clearly, he was hoping that it would be on the recommendation of the board.

15   *The Irish Times*, 19 June 1996.

The board met with Brendan Halligan for two hours on 19 June and Dineen told the media afterwards that they were 'still very unhappy with several facets' of my remuneration package. It appeared, he said, that the public pay scales had not been conformed with and this had given rise to 'grave public disquiet'. He also indicated that he hoped another board meeting the following week would reach a conclusion on the matter.

It didn't go unnoticed that the department moved to distance itself from the leaking of the second Price Waterhouse report on my remuneration, saying it had no role in the matter. The department had received one of only three copies of the report, the other two going to Dineen and the board's legal advisers.[16] Within 24 hours, Dineen felt it necessary to reiterate in a public statement that neither he nor anyone with his authority was the source of any leaked documents.

The fifth special board meeting called to investigate me was scheduled for Monday, 24 June. My asking Dineen if it would be possible to change it to the following day, because I had a prior engagement, was twisted into a report in the *Irish Times* of Friday, 21 June, that I was refusing to attend. It was yet another case of half-truths and innuendo as the fable of Eddie O'Connor became ever more sensational.

Dineen had written to me twice on Thursday, 20 June, about my attendance at the following Monday's meeting, culminating in a demand that I confirm, in writing, my agreement to attend. I found this offensive, given that I had only requested that the meeting be changed *if possible*. If he had had the courtesy to give me 24 hours to rearrange my schedule on the Monday, I would have been advising him of that privately on the Friday morning.

At the 24 June meeting I sought extra time to answer the board's questions about my package and they agreed to reconvene in a week. That turned out to be a marathon meeting on Monday, 1

16   *The Irish Times*, 20 June 1996.

July, in Dublin's Berkeley Court Hotel, starting at 2pm. I read out a 52-page statement clarifying my position and rebutting allegations of anything underhand. Nearly seven hours later it was agreed that both I and Dineen would leave the meeting and worker-director Mark Nugent, as the longest-serving remaining member of the board, was in the chair, with the other nine remaining directors. He and the other three worker-directors – P. J. Minogue, Pat McEvoy and Patrick Walsh – had played a very important role for me as the events had unfolded since April. However, some of the political appointees to the board, who didn't necessarily know much about peat, were always going to follow the government line.

The board, which adjourned that 1 July meeting until the following Thursday, was still unable to decide if my package breached government guidelines and the terms of my contract, and, if so, what to recommend to the minister.[17] After another 13 hours' deliberation on Thursday, 4 July, at a meeting that started at 9am in BNM's Newbridge HQ, they finally took the view that my package had breached government guidelines, but they were still split on whether or not to hold a vote of no confidence.[18] So there was still no resolution. A reconvening of that meeting was cancelled at the last minute by Dineen, on the instructions of the minister. He was worried that a vote of no confidence in me might be lost, which would have been further embarrassment for him. Instead, Lowry informed me that he was taking the issue to the cabinet the following Tuesday, 9 July.

It was around this time that it was announced that a senior counsel would be appointed to look into my salary.

I received a phone call from a friend of mine asking me if I wanted to stay in BNM and fight it out. I told him that I had no interest in that, and wanted to be finished with all the nonsense.

17 *The Irish Times*, 2 July 1996.
18 *The Irish Independent*, 5 July 1996.

He suggested that a deal could be organised which would allow me to leave, including a decent pension. I was very amenable to this suggestion, but I wanted my legal fees to be paid. Without the help of Frank Sowman, and, in particular, without his courage and advice, there could have been a completely different outcome.

So I resigned and got on with the next phase of my life.

CHAPTER 6

Into the Wind

'What are you going to do now, Eddie?' By the time my solicitor John Lavery asked me that question over lunch at the National Yacht Club in Dun Laoghaire towards the end of 1996, I pretty much had my mind made up.

'I think I am going to do wind,' I replied.

'How much do you need?'

'Half a million would be good,' I suggested. He rang me a week later to say he had it. John laughs now about how many of the small investors, drawn from among family and friends whom he had persuaded to back me, thought they were putting in money more as a favour to him than anything else. They had no idea that it would turn out to be the most lucrative investment they would ever make.

My friend Louis Fitzgerald, an accountant, also came on board to look after the financing and accounting side, while Brian Hurley, a lecturer in the engineering faculty at the Dublin Institute of Technology, who had been a council member of the European Wind Energy Association from 1983 to 1994, joined us as a technical expert.

After several months of a tumultuous campaign to oust me, and nine years at the helm of the peat extraction and burning behemoth, I had just finalised an exit deal from semi-state BNM, and there had been all sorts of things going through my mind about what I would do next. Due to the very public nature of my departure – it had fuelled numerous press reports and sometimes front pages since April – other people who had been wounded in life by being forced out of jobs made their way to my door to share their experiences. Very few of them seemed to have recovered; it took their lives away and left them almost defeated.

As far as I was concerned, my life's work was only beginning. You need resilience and you need people to believe in you, as John did. With 90% of my full pension being paid under the exit deal, by all standards a very good salary, Hildegarde and I were all right. It gave me the freedom to pursue my vision.

I was heading into my 50s and had spent 26 years working in electricity and energy, so I felt I knew something about that. My wife wanted me to go into IT because it seemed like everybody was moving into that area of business at the time, but I knew nothing about it. There were three factors persuading me that setting up my own renewable energy business was the way to go. One was that I had learned a vast amount about management at BNM. Before that, at the ESB, I had been doing the technology and the systems. When I went into BNM, I had to make the transition into leadership as CEO and reorganise a company that had no focus on the customer.

The second factor was that I recognised wind as a business opportunity and that it wasn't just for NGOs and do-gooders. I was convinced there had to be a bunch of products to deliver in this industry. However, I had never consciously set out in my life to make a lot of money; that is not the way I thought. I like management and I like proving a business idea.

The third factor was that renewable energy was an area where policy was being formulated and I have always had an interest in leading people in a particular direction – ever since my days as president of the students' council in UCD. The overarching driving force, though, behind forming the company that was to become Airtricity, was to prove the idea and do the right thing. And we did. It was wildly successful in every conceivable way and it changed a lot of things – not just in Ireland.

I set up Future Wind Partnership in April 1997, with John Lavery, Louis Fitzgerald and Brian Hurley as the other three partners. I owned 20%, the other three owned 10% each and the remaining investors owned 50% between them.

Wind energy was still a little-understood concept in Ireland in 1997. My plan was to bid for contracts under the Alternative Energy Requirement (AER) programme, which had been established by the government in 1996. Under its terms a power purchase agreement was to be awarded to the lowest bidder for each proposed wind farm.

We submitted carefully costed bids. We were awarded nothing. Treasury Holdings, a property development company headed by Johnny Ronan and Richard Barrett, secured everything – and ultimately built nothing that hadn't started already because they had bid too low, not knowing the industry. They were soon to find out that they couldn't build and operate at the prices secured. There were no punitive clauses in the programme to deter such unrealistic bids. In all, there were to be six versions of the AER between 1996 and 2005, before it was replaced with a renewable energy feed-in tariff, known as REFIT, in May 2006.

Globally, wind energy was a very primitive industry at the time, although Denmark was forging ahead with a much clearer, stronger political view of the importance of prioritising renewable energy. Many of the early turbine-manufacturing companies, such as Bonus, Nortank, Vestas and Nordex, were Danish companies. In 1992, the Danish government introduced a feed-in tariff, which gave wind energy providers a guaranteed price, and also set up tax incentives to encourage research and investment to boost the growth of the renewables industry. The benefits of this early political enlightenment, in a country similar in size and population to

Ireland, were to become evident over the next decade and a half. By 2007, Denmark was getting 19.7% of its energy requirements from wind power, while in Ireland that year wind was responsible for just 6.7% of gross electrical consumption.[19]

I was the only employee of the fledgling Future Wind Partnership, taking a salary of £40,000, while the other partners were in employment elsewhere, giving of their time to the company for nothing. On Monday mornings I would drive off into rural Ireland, trying to get landowners to give options over land for potential wind farms. I had kept the car I had at BNM, a 2.5-litre Ford Cosworth, as part of the exit settlement. I always got a top-of-the-range car, but never a Ferrari or a Maserati, because I wanted plenty of power, to accelerate out of trouble if necessary. I didn't really like driving but, after my time in a fur-lined mousetrap as managing director of BNM, where I had a driver, it was actually very liberating to be motoring around, meeting decent, kind people, who were largely enthusiastic about what I was proposing. I learned a lot, honing my skills in order to paint a vision for people and they went for it. I remember in particular one old couple living in County Donegal who were delighted at the prospect of somebody building something there, saying that if something like this had been going 20 years ago their children would not have had to leave. There was deep respect for what we were trying to do. After years of corporate life and moving in 'proper' circles, I was back among the real people of Ireland.

Landowners wanted to build wind farms because it was going to make them more money than they were currently earning off their land, which was poor and in elevated, exposed areas. We would do

---

19   Colin Diamond, 'The effects of Environmental Policy Integration on wind energy policy - a comparative case study of Ireland and Denmark', in *Irish Journal of Public Policy*, ISSN: 2009–1117.

a conditional lease with them to develop a site, telling them: If we get planning permission and it survives appeals, and we get a power purchase agreement and are able to build on your land, we will give you a percentage of the top line every year – 2.5% – and you take no risk whatsoever. It was a good and winning formula.

At the end of 1997 I approached Paul Dowling, a young engineer whom I had recruited to BNM and put in charge of wind there, and asked him to come on board. Paul must have believed in me because he was taking a bit of a risk leaving his permanent, pensionable job. We were both travelling around the country trying to find suitable places for developments. We would see a site on the side of the mountain, find out who the owner was and go and talk to them, telling them we had the money, although not a lot, to embark on the project. Not that it cost much to get planning permission. I remember we were down to about our last £40,000 or £50,000; when we didn't win anything in the state competition, it was either give money back to the investors or try and get some more from them. Between us we said in for a penny, in for a pound, so we got another £300,000 from them. That is very typical of a start-up, although I didn't realise it at the time. You can't anticipate success on your first venture and we had a very loyal bunch of investors.

In my early scouting for land I contacted the late John Gillespie, a friend from the ESB. He lived in Crolly, near Gweedore in County Donegal, where I had my first posting. John was quite typical of what you got in the ESB – a trade unionist, shop steward, very intelligent, ballsy and very aggressive, but he had led a strike in the ESB and had lost comprehensively. Not surprisingly he became an entrepreneur, as that is what he was by nature and had ended up in the ESB by accident. It was probably the only job available locally at the time that provided a bit of money.

He had gone on to buy a pub in Crolly where I called in to see him one day in early 1997. He suggested I should go down the road to meet a guy called Seamus Heron, whose plans for a wind farm in the area had just collapsed. In conjunction with a Northern Irish company, B9, a family-owned clean energy business based in Larne, County Antrim, he had proposed developing a wind farm at Tullytrasna, but Donegal County Council had refused planning permission. Tullytrasna was on pristine blanket bog and was declared an area of special conservation. Across the road was Culliagh, a slightly less favourable site, which Seamus wanted to develop instead, but B9 wasn't interested. I went and met Seamus in Ballybofey, near where he lived in Welchtown, and he and I agreed that we could do Culliagh.

Brian Hurley put up a wind-measuring mast on the site and we started doing all the normal things that a developer does, including recruiting an environmental consultant and getting an environmental report written before applying to Donegal County Council for planning permission. It generally takes about a year to get comprehensive wind-speed readings. Wind speed determines the amount of electricity you can make, so the readings are used to calculate the potential financial return once the plant is finished.

The granting of permission for Culliagh was appealed by a local landlord but, after An Bord Pleanála overruled his objection, we were given the green light, which got the company going. We were to build a 12MW wind farm there with Vestas V66 turbines, which were two thirds of a MW, so about 18 turbines in all.

We were also trying to do some offshore development, which Dowling had a great interest in. There are better wind speeds offshore but it costs a lot more to build there. I remember meeting Michael Woods, Minister for the Marine and Natural Resources from 1997 to 2000, and telling him I wanted to get the rights to the whole of the Irish Sea. There was no point in being modest. Woods struck me as a trifle uninterested.

However, I met a very good civil servant in his department after Woods had said we wanted a licence to develop wind in the Irish

Sea. It was uncharted territory, but this civil servant took on board what needed to be done and within a year he had produced a set of regulations for leasing areas in the Irish Sea. We got together with Dan Hannevig and his brother Chris, who had a small company based in Leeson Street, Dublin, and who were also interested in off-shore wind. Jointly we secured a development site on the Arklow Bank, a shallow-water sandbank in the Irish Sea about 10 kilometres off the east coast of Ireland, as well as another, Oriel, off the coast of Louth, south of Carlingford.

On the policy front, much of my energy was directed towards the opening up of the Irish electricity market, on foot of an EU directive, 96/92/EC. Up to then the ESB had had a complete monopoly on the generation, transmission and supply of electricity to customers, both residential and commercial. The EU Commission was demanding that the transmission of electricity be separated from the supply business and the Irish response was to split the two operations but leave them in the hands of the same owner – the state.

There wasn't much talk of green energy at the time, so we saw it as an opportunity.

I commissioned market research, which is extremely important. It doesn't have to be terribly profound but you can divide your customer base into categories, sit down with focus groups, throw out an idea and watch their reactions. We first did research with domestic customers and they were all happy with the ESB. They didn't appear to want, or see any need, to change electricity supplier. The ESB, being a semi-state, looked after them well because they were voters.

Likewise, the big business customers were well catered for because they had fantastic political power and paid discounted prices for electricity. Then we thought, how about small and medium-sized businesses? That proved to be a very different story and emerged as a potential niche for us. They really didn't like the ESB and their focus groups gave a completely different response from that expressed by domestic customers. There were about 300,000 small and medium-sized businesses in Ireland and it became clear they were the disenfranchised middle. They had bigger energy demands than households but they were charged more because they had nobody batting for them.

The big guys wielded political clout – they wouldn't locate in Ireland unless they got cheap electricity and they could also purchase in bulk. On the domestic side, the one million households had political sway through the ballot box. It was clear from our focus groups that small and medium-sized business was our target market, but how were we going to sell electricity to them?

When the Electricity Act 1999 was going through the Dáil in 1998, Mary O'Rourke was Minister for Public Enterprise. I remember ringing her about the opening up of the system.

'I have had the ESB on to me this morning and I am going to be meeting the unions this afternoon and now you're calling me and I'm pissed off!' she said.

'Really?'

'Yes. Why don't you go through the Dáil and the parliamentary procedures like you should?'

We applied ourselves to working the system, with John Lavery drafting five clauses we wanted inserted in the Act and liaising with people on the cross-party Energy Committee in the Dáil, people such as Brendan Daly, Ivan Yates, Trevor Sargent. They all thought, 'Well, why not?' We got five sections inserted at committee stage to give renewable energy providers access to the grid and access to customers. I think we were the only people looking for it and there were no objections from the ESB, who were very much focused on the generation-transmission issues. When the question of supply to customers came up, they weren't too bothered, probably thinking we posed no threat. The ESB attention was also distracted because of the criticism of Treasury Holdings. Treasury labelled the ESB Corporate Thugs, and they had a right good go at one another in the media. This was a piece of good luck and timing.

The five clauses allowed a 100% green company to sell directly to any customer of the ESB.

The construct the government had been working on initially for the opening up of the energy market was that just the top 240 (electricity demand) businesses in Ireland could change their electricity supplier; that was altered to permit a green company to sell to anybody, which allowed us to set up Airtricity. Once we were able to supply customers, we could build our own wind farms, wheel electricity across the grid and sell direct to the customer. In this way we had our own electricity supply business. We recruited marketing manager Dave Gleeson, who had worked with me in BNM, and started going to small and medium-sized businesses to sign them up.

The system was like a bank. You put green energy into the bank and the customer bought it. As long as you put in as much electricity over the year as you took out to sell to your customers, you were okay.

Culliagh was being done on a shoestring but we got a much-needed injection of capital after a chance encounter I had in the Blackrock Clinic in Dublin. I was attending for a problem with eye cataracts and when I came out, I bumped into a fellow engineer, Ciaran Blair, who was working for Tom Roche in NTR, a company building roads and toll bridges. They had been trying to develop a landfill facility in County Meath and had been turned down after a protracted planning battle.

The company was making in excess of £10 million profit from their projects, including the West and East Link toll bridges over the River Liffey in Dublin, and had been returning the cash through dividends to investors. Since they were being fully taxed on those returns, shareholders were keen for NTR to invest it in some other, more tax-efficient project, so Ciaran said they might be interested in what we were doing at Future Wind Partnership. I made an appointment to go and see Tom, who introduced me to Jim Barry, who was to do the negotiations. He had been brought in by Tom as a consultant from Bain & Company. I got Louis Fitzgerald to do all the detailed negotiation on our behalf. By late 1999 we had sold 51% of the company – renaming it Airtricity in the process – to NTR for €3 million, plus a €6 million loan to build Culliagh. This was Ireland's first wind farm built with only private finance to supply retail customers and it meant we were no longer dependent on the government's AER programmes, which were languishing amid Civil Service indecision, with nobody knowing how to proceed, or even wanting to proceed.

It was a big decision for us to sell 51% of the company but I didn't have a lot of doubts about it. NTR had the money and we had the expertise so it was a good partnership. I didn't really regret it – until possibly at the end. We couldn't really have done what we did without NTR.

NTR said if we could get full rights to the Arklow Bank development they would add another €300,000 cash to their purchase price. So, we negotiated with our partner there, Dan Hannevig, and he agreed to be bought out.

Culliagh was constructed with 50% cash from our resources and on the back of 50% debt from the Industrial Credit Corporation – a state bank put together to provide financing for industry. It was subsequently sold on to the Bank of Scotland in 2000.

At the time there was a tax-based investment scheme called the Equipment Partnership, which allowed people to invest in projects such as Culliagh in return for tax relief, giving them a return of about 21%. We went to meet with Davy's, the biggest stockbroker in town, where we were treated in a very high-handed manner by a character who told us he could redesign the investment product for half a million and then he might be able to sell it to his customers. Then we went down to NCB, with whom I had a long relationship, and met Mark Dawson, who said it was a great product and asked who he could talk to. That person was Fred Kerr, a tax partner in Ernst & Young, and we had a product that could raise money and inject it into Culliagh.

That product remained in place for a couple of years until Treasury Holdings sunk it. Richard Barrett persuaded Minister for Enterprise, Trade and Employment Mary Harney that this allowed the great unwashed to do wind business at a time that they had ambitions to take over and run the wind business in Ireland.

I remember a conversation I had with Richard Barrett where he said that he and I didn't need this scheme. He was very 'great', as they say in Ireland, with Harney at the time, and she persuaded the government to abolish the Equipment Partnership. However, by then we were out through the gap. We had built Culliagh, we had established a company supplying customers directly and we were importing electricity from Scotland into Northern Ireland, across the Moyle interconnector between Auchencrosh, South Ayrshire, and Ballycronan More in County Antrim. That was hydroelectricity, which they didn't regard as 'green' in Scotland but which was allowable as green electricity here. Scottish policymakers were trying to stimulate the production of new renewables such as wind, as they had plenty of hydro and regarded it as a traditional and therefore non-green power source. We could blend green power from Scotland with our native-produced wind and sell it to customers as green.

Future Wind Partnership/Airtricity was innovation from start to finish. It was stuff I love doing and nobody could compete at the time. Treasury tried to get developers together in 1999 to present a united front. Nobody wanted to work with them. Everybody was disgusted they had been given all the APR contracts by the government and hadn't built anything.

When we announced we were setting up a supply business, Treasury announced they were doing the same. I met Johnny Ronan later on and he admitted he couldn't even read the regulations; they didn't know what they were talking about. At the same time Denis O'Brien, who had had huge success through obtaining the country's second mobile phone licence, seemed to think he could do something similar with the electricity market opening up. It was reported that in three months he and fellow investors lost £15 million and immediately pulled out. He was probably seen as a more serious threat to the ESB at the time.

The 3MW wind farm at Corneen, near Ballyconnell in County Cavan, was our second operation in the Republic and continued our process of building a wind farm and then putting another financial package together to get the next wind farm built. It was selling power to customers that allowed us to build our wind farms. We were selling green power at a price 10% below what the ESB was charging to small and medium-sized businesses.

We learned very quickly that, despite lip service to green issues, all businesses were still making their decisions based on costs. When banks saw we were recruiting more and more customers and our cash flow was building, they would lend us more money. We went up from 55% initially, to 65% senior debt and then 75% debt on projects, reducing the equity needed. At this time Anglo Irish Bank had come on board as a lender. Although they had a disastrous collapse in 2009, I found they were very good to work with. They gave senior debt when the bigger and more established AIB and Bank of Ireland wouldn't.

Seamus Herron worked with us to develop the Meentycat wind farm near Ballybofey. Here is rural Ireland in all its glory – the names are legendary. While the collective name was Meentycat, it included the townlands of Meenahorna, Meenalaban, Ballystrang East and the Cark extension.

We had to get the power out from there and build our own sub-station, which was near to a connection point on the ESB power lines. The ESB gave us a quote of €13–14 million to build a connection from the wind farm, including the sub-station. We had a look at it ourselves and thought that was gilding the lily. We challenged their right to do that and won a signal victory, in that the regulator established the principle of contestability – that we could contest if we thought the price wasn't good value for money – and we built it ourselves for €6.5 million.

Seamus went on to develop the 25MW Kingsmountain plant in the Ox mountain range in County Sligo. We had to make quite a long connection from there to a strong point on the grid. The trouble we had with one landowner there in negotiating a wayleave nearly broke Seamus's heart. This poor man communicated directly with God who instructed him to do no business with us. Usually landowners are delighted to see you because it's a source of revenue for them and supplements their often meagre income. We used Nordex 2.5MW turbines on the Kingsmountain, which was commissioned in 2004, followed by the 15MW Gartnaneane in County Cavan at the end of that year.

When seeking planning permission for any wind project, dealing with objections forms a central chore. We have to respect the objections, provide information that helps people understand what the project is about and, hopefully, deal with their queries and objections. There was very little local opposition to either Meentycat and Kingsmountain as they were very sparsely populated areas. With onshore wind farms you often get objections from people in the community who are not benefitting from it, while their neighbours are. Managing that is part of the art of development, to make sure you can still do the project even though there are people going around alleging all kinds of issues that don't actually exist.

Some objections fall into the funny category, such as one I came across with respect to a wind farm in uplands near Edinburgh. One professorial objector claimed that the construction would release meteoric niobium into the groundwater of Edinburgh. A million people would die as a result. I had to admire the imagination that led to that comment, outrageous though it was.

There was a clear chain of command and common purpose at Airtricity. When I was working in BNM, it was always open to question who the owner was – the civil servants, the minister or the Dáil? Did it exist primarily to provide employment in the Midlands or to make a profit? Such double 'bottom lines' are nonsense, and they really don't work. In business it's simple: you go out there and make a profit or make cash. However, profits are a theoretical construct, cash is real. When you own a business, the thing you can't do is run out of cash. So many profitable companies have failed because the cash hasn't come in. You only have to think about credit and customers will take it. My advice to all small start-up companies is get your cash: nobody is a customer until they pay for the service or product you sell. If one guy's extended credit terms could run your company out of business, don't provide the service or product unless he's paid for it – however well you think you know the person.

We went into Northern Ireland very quickly, first establishing Tappaghan Mountain wind farm in County Fermanagh in 2005. In the early days I recruited the best managers I could to build the company, starting with Paul Dowling, and then Mark Ennis, who, in 2001, had stepped down as chief executive of the Northern Ireland packaging company Boxmore (formerly managed by his father Dr Harold Ennis) after it had been acquired by the US packaging company Chesapeake. The family hadn't wanted to sell Boxmore, but the £241 million offer was too good a deal to turn down.

Other early appointments included our marketing manager, Dave Gleeson. We used the OCEAN psychological (also known as psychometric) test in our recruitment, on which I elaborate later in this book, and got the brightest people.

Meanwhile, Airtricity had also crossed over to Scotland, where we hired Steve Cowie, who had run Scottish Power's wind farm operations for the previous eight years,[20] to lead our business there. He was a very clever engineer. Our first development was a 12-turbine, 24MW plant at Ardrossan in north Ayrshire, which was commissioned in February 2004.

The British government had tried competitive tenders (called the Non Fossil Fuel Obligation or NOFFO) in the early days of renewable energy and they were a complete disaster. As Treasury did in Ireland, people bid too low because they didn't know the risks. The British government then went for the ROC (Renewable Obligation Certificate) scheme, which was very similar to what they had in Texas and obliged electricity supply companies to have a percentage of their power coming from green sources. The ROC was worth 4p a unit, with a secondary ROC worth an additional 50%, so there was a subsidy of 6p. The price of electricity was about 5p a unit so you would be getting about 11p per unit.

We saw that as a fantastic system and went for it with Barclays, the only bank that backed us, and made great returns out of building Ardrossan. Going into it, our business model was to fund the build programme with 75–80% senior debt. The rest would be our own equity. However, with mezzanine financing in there, you really had 90% debt.

The amount of debt you can get into a project is driven by your need to pay the bank its interest and its capital repayment – a bit like a mortgage. The cash flow needed to be 1.3 above that, in case there was a dip in wind speed in some months. It worked extremely well for us. The payments we received for electricity sales from Ardrossan were so high that within two or three years we could

---

20   *The Scotsman*, 5 August 2005.

secure 130% debt. We had a huge competitive advantage by being innovative. There had not been a lot of talent around in the energy industry at that time, as most of the big utilities are public monopolies, which don't foster innovation and risk-taking. Whereas in the private sector, once you make something work, you get copied straight away so there is no protection from anybody. You have to get used to that and competition makes you perform much better.

Our next development, the Braes of Doune in Stirlingshire, was a 36-turbine, 72MW wind farm, which opened in 2007. Other Scottish projects included what was at the time to be the biggest wind farm on land, nearly 500MW, in the upper Clyde, between the towns of Biggar and Moffat in South Lanarkshire. There was a lot of opposition when we unveiled our plans for it in 2003. A very active protest group, ACE Environmental Watch, named after three local towns – Abington, Crawford and Elvanfoot – campaigned very vigorously against it. They even got naturalist David Bellamy to organise and attend a march against the wind farm and bussed in other objectors. I had sent Cameron Smith and Pauline Alison around Abington, Crawford and Elvanfoot, knocking on doors telling people about the proposed wind farm, and they found that few of the folks they met at the doorsteps were objectors to it. We knew that it was really all down to ACE. For our part, we liaised with local businesses about the huge economic benefits it would bring to the area, with up to 750 jobs in the construction phase and up to 46 local jobs to maintain it.[21]

A public inquiry into the plans started in August 2006, by which time we had reduced the proposed number of turbines from 200 to 160, because of the higher capacity turbines that had become available during the development process. At the inquiry it transpired ACE had only a handful of paid-up members (five in all), people who didn't want change and who were able to hold up this huge

21   *Carluke Gazette*, 23 August 2006.

clean energy project. The Clyde wind farm finally got planning consent from the Scottish Ministers in the summer of 2008, after Airtricity had been sold to Scottish and Southern Energy.

Back home we had a falling-out in 2003 with the operators of the national transmission grid. EirGrid had been established in 2001 to manage and operate the national transmission grid but it took five years before it became a stand-alone semi-state company. In 2003, while still functioning effectively as an arm of the ESB, EirGrid persuaded the energy regulator of the time, Tom Reeves, to stop new connections to the grid because of 'technical issues'. At a penetration of 2% they alleged that renewable energy was destabilising the grid.

We went after them aggressively because they were taking away our careers and spoiling the environment, instead of behaving as engineers should, designing new solutions; they were just behaving conservatively and not looking at the bigger pollution aspect of electricity generation.

At times like that, the policy aspect of a role like mine is very important. I learned this mostly from Brendan Halligan when working with him at BNM. At this stage Airtricity would have been seen as a venture that was clearly working and various other people were also developing wind farms, so politicians were listening. The moratorium was lifted in May 2005, thereby ending a period of uncertainty for wind-energy development. It wasn't until 2006 that EirGrid became totally independent of the ESB.

As Airtricity grew we were able to meet our customer demand, not just from our own plants and by importing hydro power from Scotland, but also with hydro bought in from France, across the interconnector from France to England, across England to Northern Ireland and down to our customer base. We were continually innovating and doing things nobody else was doing – and winning.

We were early adopters, and blessed with a very dedicated and talented team of people. We managed to make a profit on our output to the customer, and still undercut the ESB by 10%. We held on to all of our wind farms, and our prices increased every year. All of that meant that our share price went up 54% a year on average over the 11 years. Every euro invested got 73 cents back.

By comparison, the US NASDAQ, despite a peak in 2000, actually fell by 11% in that time, while the Dow Jones was up 25%. Despite highs in 1999 and 2007, London's FTSE 100 fell by 2.9% during those 11 years. Ireland's ISEQ, despite a peak in 2007, fell 20% in the same period. We beat them all by an enormous margin.

CHAPTER 7

Airtricity Crosses the Atlantic

Our first foray into the US was when we sent Declan
Flanagan there in 2003. Declan had been recruited from
the regulatory department of Irish business organisation IBEC in 2000. He was keen to go and based himself first in
Boston, where he had personal connections. From there he moved
to Minneapolis in Minnesota, which was close to where wind energy was taking off, and then on to Chicago where he set up an office
and we began to make contacts. One of the thousands of cultural
differences between here and the US is that they all go to confer-
ences. If you have 5,000 people at a conference in Europe, you are
doing really well. If you have fewer than 25,000 in America you
would think you were doing badly. One of the reasons capitalism
works over there is that they share information all the time. They're
very outward looking – networking is part of what they do and
they'll travel within the US at the drop of a hat.

We sent Martin McAdam over there in 2004. Martin is a really,
really bright guy, who had come to work with me in the ESB, and
was 'shit hot' at computers. When he went to the US he recommended Texas, but Declan didn't want to go there; he thought we
were too late. In fact, Texas ultimately was where we did nearly all
our work. In 2004 we hired John Fedorko, former head of Nordex
North America, to lead our entry into the Texas market. That same
year, Ciaran O'Brien relocated from the Dublin office to become
head of finance for North America.

I loved doing business in Texas, where wind farms were being seen as a way to revive the local economy. You walk into towns in West Texas and the stoop is falling down and all the talent has left. Once upon a time it might have been a railhead. Roscoe is such a place. The Union Pacific railroad runs right through the town, which has a population of less than 1,500. We were building a wind farm of up to 1,000MW there. Typically, you go to the local mayor for planning permission. He would be friendly, courteous and straight to the point:

'So, you want to build a 500MW farm?'

'Yes'

'Is it going to be profitable?'

'Absolutely, very profitable.'

'What's wrong with 1,000MW then?'

That's your planning permission, straight away. Five minutes. If you want to do business, they're there to do business.

Texas is a fabulous place, with a population of more than 28 million. It would be one of the richest countries in the world if it was an independent state and they are incredibly pro-business. I remember making a speech in New York, during which I quite deliberately started (because you have to keep the attention of the audience even if it means making a joke about yourself): 'Down in the independent Republic of Texas … Very sorry, in the State of Texas … ', I continued.

This big guy came up to me afterwards:

'Hey, son, no problem talking about the independent empire of Texas, that is just the way we are.' That is the way they think. The Texas State Capitol building is taller than the US Capitol in Washington DC.

When you are in another country, I really think you should try to bring together a sub-board that will help you to understand the culture and politics there. In our early days in the US, we had dealings with Pat Wood III, head of the Federal Electricity Regulatory Corporation (FERC), the federal body that looks after all transmission in the US and lays down the rules. After he retired from FERC in 2005, I proposed to Pat that he could chair our sub-board, which he did until the company was sold in 2007.

Pat Wood had studied law in Harvard; he was a very bright guy and a Catholic – on his honeymoon he and his wife Kathleen went to meet the Pope. That is why he took a special interest in us, being Irish and Catholic, not that I ever bothered to let him know what my views on religion were. Before he became chairman of FERC, Pat had been appointed in 1995 by Texas Governor George W. Bush to head the Public Utility Commission of Texas. His task was to liberate power and telecom customers from the control of a monopoly utility. The resulting Electricity Regulatory Company of Texas (ERCOT) is regarded as facilitating one of the most vigorous and competitive energy markets in the whole of the US.

There were three regulators in ERCOT and they were never allowed to have a private meeting between themselves. If they were ever together there had to be a public audience. Talk about transparency! There was no 'old boys' network'; the rules were non-discriminatory, with a focus on 'open for business' to all.

Pat told me that on one occasion when he was leaving after discussing business with Governor Bush, Bush said:

'Hey, Pat.'

'Yes, Governor?'

'We like wind, Pat.'

'Excuse me, Governor?'

'We like wind, Pat.'

'Oh, I see what you mean, Governor, thanks very much.'

So, they got wind farms going in Texas and they are now by far the largest US state with wind. The renewable energy industry became very sophisticated there and the world has copied it to a certain extent.

Airtricity opened an office in Austin. We placed a gigantic order with GE for 1,000MW.

We became quite a significant company very quickly because we caught this wave and it was working really well. We had to pay $60 million for the turbines two years before delivery, another $60 million six months later and a further $120 million the year before we got the turbines. We were covering the entire working capital: it was such a profitable business for GE. They had entered the market by buying the wind-turbine manufacturing assets of Enron Wind Corporation in 2002, after its parent company Enron had filed for bankruptcy in December 2001. Enron's collapse led to the demise of Arthur Andersen, one of the most reputable multinational accounting firms and Enron's auditors.

Enron Wind had, in 1997 bought both Tacke Windtechnik, a German turbine-manufacturing firm, and the California-based Zond, which was then one of the largest US manufacturers of wind turbines.

There were cracking wind speeds in West Texas and the Panhandle. A traditional grid is only capable of taking so much wind. Traditional grids were built for fossil-fired plant, so large power stations were constructed, usually remote from cities, and very high-capacity transmission lines were built to carry the power to the cities. In all countries, and in Texas as well, there is some unused capacity on these transmission lines. This gets used up in the early exploitation of wind.

In Texas the grid was almost used up by 2009. In 2006, the regulator had started a process to set up special renewable energy zones. All companies were invited to make submissions as to where these special zones would be located and what transmission lines would be needed to transport the electricity to centres of population. Their welcoming and open attitude is very hard to reconcile with

President Trump's desire to close the Mexican border. I can't imagine many Republicans in Texas want that — they have no problem with outsiders coming in. If you're rich, you use Mexican labour because it's cheap, and there is full employment. I regard Trump as a dealmaker rather than a businessman. He doesn't seem to know that politicians use their only tool, words, to communicate a vision or an idea. He uses words as a battering ram to hammer everybody into submission before he goes to deal with them. After a brief consultation period, the regulator came up with proposals to build four competitive renewable energy zones — CREZs. Private companies were invited to compete to build new transmission lines, which would open up areas for development that hadn't been able to accommodate any wind up until then.

The four CREZs were built by 2012.

We did a plant in Munnsville, upstate New York, in a joint venture with Joe Kennedy, Robert Kennedy's son. It is where I encountered the concept of not-for-profit for the first time. In 1979, Joe had founded Citizens Energy, a non-profit organisation to provide low-income families with heating oil at a discounted price. He then spent nearly 14 years in the US Congress, having won a Democratic seat in Massachusetts after the retirement of Democrat Thomas 'Tip' O'Neill, the House Speaker. In 1999 he returned to Citizens Energy, which had been run by his brother Michael in his absence, and led the firm into the renewable-energy industry. That was how our paths crossed in 2003/04.

Three of us went to meet him in his office in Boston. He clearly enjoyed the cachet of being Robert Kennedy's son and his office was decorated with wall-to-wall photos of himself with dignitaries, from the Pope to Nelson Mandela — it was hilarious. I have never before seen four walls that were completely full of photographs of one person.

We were asked to wait and were sitting outside his office when we heard a roar. The young woman behind the desk motioned us into the office. He had two flunkies with him. He'd crack a joke and they would burst out laughing. He would then make a cutting action with his hands and the lads would stop laughing, just like in the movies. Joe took out a sandwich while we were with him and said, 'You don't mind if I eat here, do you? You get all kinds of bums coming through here.' He was eating his sandwich as he told us how business was and that he was importing oil from Nigeria. It was a surreal experience and I fell out of the place laughing. He was all bluster and a gigantic ego, with not an awful lot behind it, whereas his father was a genuinely talented man and could have been president.

Joe rang me in New York later on, as I was walking down the street on a cold day after a meeting. He says: 'Eddie, I am very nervous about this Munsville project, is it going to work?'

I said, 'Of course it's going to work, no problem whatsoever.'

'I don't know about that,' he replied.

I said 'Joe, if you're worried about it, I'll buy you out.' I knew exactly how to keep him on board.

He stuck with it after that; it was a good project and has been built.

I remember meeting a crowd over in Minnesota, actually probably the north of Iowa, where there is a large number of wind farms. It is called the top of Iowa. They told us about these 60% capacity factors they were getting. I said, 'We regard it as very good if we get 40%'.

Of course, you might be able to get 60% from one turbine, but you couldn't do it across the board. One particularly colourful character in that group had been a roadie with the 1960s American rock band the Grateful Dead and was now into wind farms. I remember him talking about touring and saying: 'Australia? We were there for three months, so they tell me, I don't recall too much of it.' You meet all kinds of people on this quest.

We tried to build in Idaho, which is a very interesting place, full of natural beauty and great for fishing. We would have loved to have built there but we just couldn't get the turbines in at the right price. It's a very long state, very sparsely populated, and that was what sunk our proposal.

You could raise equity capital in America because of the production tax credit system, making it so much easier to do business there than anywhere else. By the time Airtricity's North American operation was sold to Eon for a billion dollars in October 2007, the company was operating in nine states, with a concentration in Texas and the north-east. We had more than 75 employees working there, with offices in Chicago, Austin and Toronto. At that stage Airtricity North America had commissioned 124MW, completed construction of a further 90MW, with an additional 370MW under construction and 704MW in final stages of development backed by firm orders for turbines for delivery in 2008 through early 2009. With an additional 6,500MW under development, the company was well positioned to capitalise on the significant growth of wind power in the US and Canada. It would not have been my choice to sell our US interests; I liked going to the US and I liked doing business there, but the Airtricity board wanted to sell the US division separately, before putting up the rest of the company for sale.

CHAPTER 8

Renewable Energy Systems – Bigger, Better, Cheaper

This book exists because there is a need for a revolution in energy supply. There has to be complete movement to renewable energy and the non-use of fossil fuels for energy purposes. The principal energy technology in a non fossil-fired world is electricity.

Technology is never value free: it exists because someone puts a value on developing it. With me it's all about doing away with the production of CO_2 for energy purposes. I discovered in 1989 that greenhouse gases, mostly CO_2, were trapping more energy in the atmosphere than in pre-industrial times. I was Ireland's leading polluter at the time, emitting 10 million tonnes per year at BNM. There is a concentration of 415 PPMV (parts per million by volume – a measure of the quantity of CO_2 in the atmosphere) now as against 270 in pre-industrial times. The atmosphere is capturing the energy equivalent of four Hiroshima atomic bombs each second. In a report published by Greenpeace in February 2020 for the Centre for Research on Energy and Clean Air it was estimated that the current cost to the people of the world of this excessive CO_2 is $2.9 trillion. We added between 33 and 36.8 billion tonnes of CO_2 to the atmosphere in 2019, so the cost per tonne of CO_2 is $79. The inability of the world's economists to put pollution at the centre of political economy debate and budget action is puzzling.

Once I found out about CO_2, I dedicated my life to removing this scourge from the human firmament. In a world that is increasingly technological, and sometimes obscurely so, it is refreshing to realise that decarbonisation relies on two apparently simple generation technologies: wind and solar photovoltaic (PV). The solution to the problem is simple: use electricity for all energy needs and make all electricity from wind and solar.

Modern wind generation began in Denmark with the Gedser machine, installed in 1955.

All modern wind turbines are based on the original design of the Gedser machine. It has three blades, all upwind – facing into the wind as distinct from being behind the turbine from the direction in which the wind is blowing. The Gedser machine didn't need maintenance for the first 12 years of its life. The blades were fixed in position, so that when the wind blew at a stronger speed than the blades were designed for, they automatically stalled. This type of machine is known as 'stall regulated'. It was the precursor to the more sophisticated pitch-regulated blades, which came along later.

When we built Ireland's first wind farm in 1992, the size of the turbines was 250kW (0.25MW), with an experimental 400kW machine. Now the size of on-land wind turbines is 5MW, larger to a factor of 20. Offshore the standard size is 8–12MW.

At the time of writing Mainstream is building 1500MW of wind energy installations between Senegal, Egypt and Chile. The cost in Egypt and Chile is 4.1 $ cents per unit of electricity. As turbines get bigger the electricity they produce gets cheaper. The reason for this is twofold. Firstly, the towers are much taller, so they access wind whose speed is higher. The nacelles of the turbines we installed in Bellacorick are at a height of 40 metres. The ones we are installing in Chile are some 130 metres tall. Secondly, the cost of wind turbines reflects the length of the blades, whereas the energy capture is proportional to blade length squared.

The wind turbines are not just making cheaper electricity. They are making more grid-friendly electricity. Older turbines were connected to the low voltage distribution system and were seen as negative load, not as generators of electricity. When I heard of negative load for the first time I was puzzled. What did it mean?

These early turbines were local and generated small quantities of electricity. They supplied local markets and the electricity was not transmitted over long distances. When a fault occurred in the transmission system, local towns, houses and businesses were disconnected from the electricity system until the fault was repaired and the transmission system re-energised. The older local wind farms would also be turned off when this kind of interruption to electricity supply happened. It seemed contradictory to me to cut off a source of electricity when it was most needed. I'm sure safety was a concern, as well as the central control centre's inability to monitor and regulate a generation source that was so remote from them.

Modern turbines are connected to the high-voltage transmission system and are regarded as full-throttle power stations. One of the main differences between this arrangement and the former one is that modern wind farms must remain connected to the transmission system when there is a fault. The wind turbine manufacturers had to change the design of the turbine controls – and a new suite of control equipment called 'fault ride through' was introduced. This brought wind turbines in line with normal power stations, which are required to continue producing electricity if at all possible.

Capacity factors of wind turbines, largely on account of the move offshore, are now in the order of 50%. With floating technology coming along at quite a pace, soon wind speeds of 11 metres/second will be capable of being accessed. This will yield capacity factors of 65%. These wind speeds and accompanying capacity factors are experienced off the west coasts of Ireland and Scotland. On land, a really good wind farm would have a capacity factor of 35–40%.

The latest iteration in wind turbine design will allow turbines to be built in water depths greater than 60 metres, which is the limit for those with fixed foundations.

As an example of technology evolution, 40 different designs for floating platforms are currently being developed. Two of these have been installed. In 2017 Equinor installed five 5MW floating turbines in 95–120 metres of water in the Buchan Deep off the east coast of Scotland. They have worked brilliantly, surviving 8-metre waves and winter storms. Throughout, the deflection of the nacelle, 98 metres above the water level, never exceeded 3 degrees.

The other design is deployed off Portugal, and was developed by Principle Power. It has three floating elements in the base, as illustrated below.

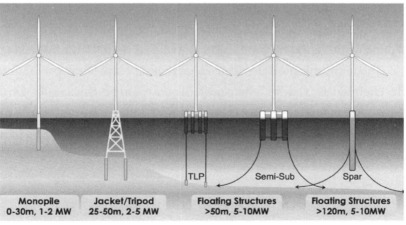

Wind turbines make electricity without burning fuel. The temperature at which they operate is therefore at or near ambient temperature. This means they have a long life, and don't suffer from any of the faults inherent in high-temperature and high-pressure fossil- or nuclear-fired generating plant.

'Availability' is a key measurement that applies to all generators, whether fossil-fired or renewable. When we installed the first wind turbine generators the manufacturers guaranteed 95% availability. Now they guarantee 97% or 98%, and operators are disappointed if it is not higher than that.

The story of solar PV is equally or even more dramatic. It was very expensive up to 2009, until the Chinese began to mass produce the silicon-based modules. Another factor in reducing the price was the rapid roll-out of solar PV, made possible by the generous support scheme introduced by Germany.

Solar PV used to be fixed flat surfaces facing roughly in the direction of the sun. Now the panels are installed on single axis tracking systems, which follow the sun from sunrise to sunset. Output from solar farms has been increased by using bi-facial panels. If the solar plant is installed on white surfaces there is considerable reflection of radiation back up to the underside of the panel. This stratagem has further increased the output.

In an unexpected development, we are beginning to see floating PV farms on lakes, reservoirs and the tailing ponds from mines.

The net result of all this innovation is that solar PV is producing electricity at incredibly low prices. In desert areas, for large farms, prices are as low as 1.5 $ cents per unit of electricity. In Chile in 2016 Mainstream bid 2.96 $ cents per unit, and didn't win. A competitor bid 2.91 $ cents.

Two revolutionary aspects are associated with all these developments:

1. The fuel is free. Capital costs are high particularly in the case of wind, but once built, the fuel costs nothing. Bellacorick, where we built Ireland's first wind farm in 1992, is still running with no fuel cost.

2. The CIA has published their estimates for the levelised cost of a unit of electricity (LCOE) for coal-fired plant being built today. The LCOE is calculated over the lifetime of the coal-fired plant. On average globally this cost is 9.2 $ cents per unit. No allowance for pollution abatement is included in this figure. If pollution were to be charged the cost added to the pure coal-fired electricity price would be 8.17 $ cents, so if a true price were to be charged for this electricity, it would cost 9.2 + 8.17 $ cents = 17.37 $ cents.

Wind costs 3.5–6 $ cents per unit. Solar PV costs 1.5–5 $ cents. There are no pollution charges.

No technology comes without disadvantages. Wind and solar are no exception. Wind is variable in output, and depends on the strength of the wind in the vicinity of the wind farm. It is not possible to dial it up or down as can be done with fossil-fired plant. Solar only makes electricity during daylight hours. It is truly intermittent. The presence of clouds also affects the amount of electricity that a solar PV plant can make.

These are other issues to be dealt with.

Storage of electricity is becoming necessary as the penetration of renewables increases. The traditional method of storing electricity is pumped storage. This involves a two-lake arrangement, with one lake much higher than the other. At times of cheap electricity water is pumped from the bottom to the top lake. When there is a shortage the valves are opened and the water flows down and drives the turbines. These pumped storage arrangements are expensive to build and operate at an efficiency of 70%. What this means is that if 100MWh were used to pump the water up to the top, 70MWh would flow into the grid. Globally there is some scope to build more of these, but they will make a small contribution in a completely decarbonised sustainable world.

Modern storage of electricity is via lithium ion batteries, which are used in electric vehicles. Lithium ion batteries work extremely well in cars, with 90% of the energy put into the battery being used to drive the car. This contrasts with the internal combustion engine, whose efficiency is much lower, at 15–22%. The great news is that the price is falling almost as fast as that of solar PV, some 18% per annum.

Tesla founder Elon Musk built an electricity storage system in Southern Australia, using lithium ion batteries (110MWh). It paid for itself in five months. Musk guaranteed to install the plant before 1 November 2017. It he didn't make this date, he wouldn't charge for it. Needless to say it came in on time.

I am not sure how long the lithium ion battery system will be the most cost-effective system. There are many other electricity storage systems being designed and, indeed, invented currently. I would not be surprised to see cheaper and more effective batteries come along on our pathway to decarbonisation.

No matter how much electricity storage there is, we still need a far more substantial grid to capture the huge amount of additional electricity we will need and transmit it from the areas of abundant wind and solar to consumers. Elsewhere I describe how much electricity will be needed when all fossils are replaced and all heating and transport are electrified. Demand in Europe will more than double, from 3100TWh to 7800 TWh. Most of this electricity will be generated remotely from where it is manufactured. This will require the building of the Supergrid, which

- collects the electricity from where it can be generated most cheaply;

- transmits to the centres of population;

- links the great northern wind resource to the huge southern solar one;

- balances the wind and the solar output. During the summer when the sun is shining strongly in the south the wind is weakest in the north. Likewise, in winter, when crashing storms assail the north, the sun is at its weakest in the south.

- cuts down on the need for electricity storage and minimises the building of generating plant;

- will make Europe completely independent of other nations for its energy supply. In current terms this will save €350 billion per annum.

Even with electricity storage and the Supergrid, there may be times when demand for electricity across Europe exceeds supply. Even with a very well-designed system, faults can occur, or natural disasters can interfere with a region's or country's supply. The way to deal with this eventuality is to have demand side management in place. The technology to do this already exists. Nearly all freezers could be switched off and there would be no loss of function. The same applies to many fridges. Premises heating could be reduced by 1 degree and scarcely anyone would notice the difference.

CHAPTER 9

The Sale of Airtricity and the Founding of Mainstream

The decision to sell off Airtricity's North American interests was just a prelude to the sale of the holding company. We were at the height of offshore development and a very high cash-yielding proposition.

The challenge of being a utility is that you're always running out of money. We were constantly having to raise money for the next project or group of projects. The majority shareholder, NTR, was keen to get its return on its investment in the company and decided first to sell off the US subsidiary. When E.ON came in with a billion-dollar cheque and bought Airtricity North America lock, stock and barrel, we had nothing left there. By the time that sale closed in December 2007, with the proceeds ploughed back into the company, the rest was up for sale.

I tried to buy it but I didn't get going quick enough. It all happened relatively quickly and I wasn't able to put together the equity capital to buy it. I wrote to the board on 14 December 2007, telling them I wanted to lead a management buy-out, but at that stage there had already been other firm bids. I believed the company had been undervalued and had much greater potential than was being recognised if the €1.8 billion offer from Scottish and Southern General were to be accepted.

I reckoned, considering it included €0.86 billion cash, it was worth about three times that. At time of sale, Airtricity was involved in operating 19 windfarms: 13 in the Republic of Ireland, two in Northern Ireland and four in Scotland.

I, of course, had to recuse myself from the board's final discussion and decision on 4 January 2008 to sell to SSE. The board was uncomfortable with running a supply business in Ireland, but it was our supply business that got SSE interested. (We had 40,000 customers at that stage and SSE Airtricity now has more than 900,000.) All the other board members were in favour of the sale and thought I was looking a gift horse in the mouth.

In hindsight, it was quite a good decision to sell at that time. I don't know whether anybody could see the global financial collapse coming but I don't think so. However, the board was following the business wisdom that you always do commercial deals as quickly as you can because circumstances can change overnight. It was just over two months later that the New York investment bank Bear Stearns failed, followed by the collapse of Lehmann Brothers the following September. It was financial blackout in Europe for five or six years after that.

On the break-up of Airtricity, the CEO of SSE said if I wanted to stay on I could, 'but I suspect you don't want to'.

'You're right about that,' I replied.

I didn't need any time for reflection after the sale of Airtricity. I knew what I wanted to do. It wasn't money that was driving me on, it was all about making electricity sustainably, and stopping CO_2 emissions. Being an extrovert, I wanted my contribution at that level to be seen.

One of the big motivators when I came out of BNM was the belief that I wasn't being recognised for what had been accomplished there. I was determined to show the detractors and begrudgers that what happened to BNM during my leadership spell there didn't happen by accident.

I didn't feel the same compulsion to prove myself after Airtricity. My track record spoke for itself – not once but twice I had led companies to success. This time it was the deep conviction of the need to make the world more sustainable that motivated me. I thought, and still think, that the world is on a once-off transition to sustainability. It needed people of conviction to lead it, and allied to this belief we now had the experience of a start-up (Airtricity) behind us.

After a decade of success with Airtricity, I was approaching my 60s and was of the view that this business was only starting on a global basis. It wasn't the end, or the beginning of the end, it was only the end of the beginning of the transition to sustainability.

My second-in-command at Airtricity, Paul Dowling, could see himself becoming chief executive of a large company after the buyout and my inevitable departure. He stayed on to be that chief executive and then found out that there was no intention of having a meaningful chief executive here as the Irish operation was effectively a branch office of a Scottish company. He had no particular qualifications in office politics and in a big bureaucracy like that you need a PhD in office politics to survive. He lasted about two years there and had a year as director of strategy with SSE. In 2012 he became chairman of Island Renewable Energy, at a time when Louis Fitzgerald and Denis O'Sullivan, who had been involved with me in Airtricity from the beginning, became investors in it.

My position with Airtricity was terminated on 1 February 2008. It was the first time in my life I had serious wealth, having netted about €44 million from the sale of Airtricity, but I had no interest in retiring to luxuriate in fripperies. I spent a couple of weeks, if that, holidaying in Canada with my wife and family. We have good friends in British Columbia, where we went skiing in the Sun Peaks resort, and then I came back to set up Mainstream.

My founding partner was the Airtricity corporate finance secretary, Fintan Whelan, who had been let go by SSE because he had publicly aligned himself with me in the management buy-out proposal. It was Fintan who came up with the name 'Mainstream' for the new company, which was incorporated in March 2008. I thought it was a great name because it signalled our intent to take renewables mainstream. I wanted to take the proposition global – so far it had been confined to certain countries in Europe and the US, and I knew the renewables industry was going to spread to the whole world.

John Lavery was still by my side too, although he was straddling both sides of the fence because, as Airtricity company secretary, he was still finalising the sale deal while helping with the Mainstream start-up. However, there was no conflict of interest and he was never an employee of Airtricity.

A lot of people didn't like me doing this again. These were people who had made a lot of money out of Airtricity. I don't know what their problem was or what was in their heads. Maybe they thought I should go off and lie on a beach and enjoy my wealth at my leisure. But that's not who I am, and fulfilling my vision for global renewable energy was still very much unfinished business.

There had been no question of me coming out of Airtricity with 'golden handcuffs'. The company had been bought by a mighty corporation and I don't think they were too worried about what I might do as an individual. Perhaps they regarded me as just the figurehead and thought that my management team had done all the work. It is my style to delegate massively and I spend a lot of time thinking about doing things. Nobody wants to work with control freaks. (I did once work with such a person and it was a nightmare – he turned off a whole department.)

However, there was a clause in my resignation agreement that prevented my setting up a company to build wind farms in Ireland and supplying customers within the following two years. However, there was nothing to stop me forming a development company to build wind farms abroad.

Brendan Halligan was running his public affairs company, CIPA, from offices in the top half of a Georgian house on Baggot Street, and had invited me and my secretary, Marian Shanahan, to come and work there. A wonderful boardroom, only occasionally used for big meetings, was put at our disposal, and we moved in with our laptops and mobile phones. I was also able to use a small room adjoining Brendan's office on the top floor for talking to people privately as I started building my team for Mainstream.

I wanted to start off with as many skills within my new company as possible. I was particularly interested in Airtricity's off-shore team in the UK, as I reckoned offshore development was a big bet and one I wanted to take. While my exit deal had also included a 'non-poaching' agreement, there was nothing to stop any of my former staff ringing me up to inquire if I might have a job for them. It was not as if the new owners had been making them feel particularly valued. The chief executive of SSE had been asked at a general meeting of all staff if he saw the value of Airtricity as being the staff or the assets. Without any hesitation he said it was the assets. Joining me in Mainstream wasn't a hard move for a lot of them. What's more, they had all done very well out of the sale of Airtricity because they all had share options. The number of Airtricity shares granted to the employees depended on their level of seniority in the company but many received enough to buy houses. Up to 700 employees shared €100 million between them.

The head of offshore wind development, Torben Anderson from Denmark, and about 30 other people jumped ship from Airtricity to join me. Of course, there were some people who wanted to come with us whom we did not particularly want, so there was, inevitably, splintering of relationships in the aftermath.

However, it was somebody I hadn't worked with before, Andy Kinsella, who was my first target. He had impressed me in his career – he had worked in Siemens and in GE and had been in and out of the ESB – effectively running the whole generational set-up there. I didn't know it at the time but he was looking for a change too. Although we had only met occasionally, I admired his energy and enthusiasm. I used jokingly to call him Andy Garcia, as his slicked-back hair reminded me of the actor.

When I rang him from the office on Baggot Street early in 2008, Andy had seen the telephone number beginning 696 come up on his phone display and said 'you must be near here'. He was just around the corner in the ESB head office on Fitzwilliam Street. I told him that while I could stay on in Airtricity, I was leaving to set up a new business and asked would he be interested in coming in as a director?

'You could not have rung me at a better time,' Andy replied. Having left ESB International once to work in private business, with Siemens, he had found semi-state company politics harder to take on his return.

Andy walked around to the office in Baggot Street and sat down with me for more than three hours. At the end of it, he looked at me and said:

'It all sounds very interesting and exciting, but how are you going to fund this?'

I explained that I was going to get about €55 million out of my share of the sale of Airtricity and I expected to have €44 million after paying tax. I was going to put in €30 million the following week as equity to found the company.

Andy reached across the table to shake my hand and said, 'Count me in. If you're that committed to the venture, I'm with you.'

When Andy had agreed to go back to the ESB, he took out the reference to giving notice in the contract before he signed and returned it. That was never spotted, so he didn't have to give any notice. However, for obvious reasons, he wouldn't leave the ESB until the medical for Mainstream had been completed, and that took a while at our end. As soon as he got the medical all-clear,

Andy left the ESB on the Thursday of the May bank holiday week-end in 2008 and started in Mainstream on the following Tuesday. The day after he handed in his resignation letter, the head of ESB Power Generation, Pat Doherty, rang him to say that he was very sorry but they would have to restrict his access within the company while he worked out his notice, as is normal procedure to protect commercial sensitivities when somebody is leaving.

'Pat, I am not there any more,' Andy said.

'What do you mean, you're not here any more? You have three months' notice on your contract.' 'No I don't,' said Andy.

I know Andy admired how I showed the courage of my con-victions, that I was always willing to take a stand on what I be-lieved and to ignore the cynics and those laughing down their sleeves. Although we are different personalities, if Andy believes in something, he too will work very hard to go after it – as he was to prove with Neart na Gaoithe. From the moment he joined Mainstream, I gave him the freedom to do what he is good at and had no doubt, a decade later, that he was the right person to take over from me as CEO when I stepped back from that role in September 2017.

The €30 million I invested to start Mainstream was a lot of capi-tal but I did not know the big crash was coming. As I and the team had a good reputation within the renewables industry, Barclays in-vested another €20 million, so we had a good fund to start off with, but we had no developments or property. We had a close look first at what might be possible to develop here in Ireland, but when I consulted Seamus Heron, who had started us all off in Airtricity, he told me he reckoned Ireland was all done. I don't think he was far wrong – in terms of onshore anyway – and I certainly couldn't disprove his assessment at the time. In hindsight, we should have explored more options instead of going back to the US, which had been very profitable for us with Airtricity.

The US was to prove a bit of a disaster for Mainstream. The combination of the financial crisis and the huge expansion of shale gas extraction, enabled by hydraulic fracturing techniques, known as 'fracking', had negatively affected the economic conditions for renewable energy development. I won't say we were lucky to have survived what turned out to be a very difficult period after our start-up, because we made all the correct big decisions, but we could have done with less of the chaff and been more selective in what Mainstream chose to do.

We would have liked to build more in Texas, but capacity on the grid ran out, and a production tax credit came to an end. We also struggled to find talented managers to run our US operations.

CHAPTER 10

Neart na Gaoithe

Sometimes a story within a story encapsulates a lifelong philosophy. A wind farm off the east coast of Scotland provided one such saga. If you believe in something, you challenge the status quo, you keep going and find your way around every obstacle. That's the way I live my life and I have always encouraged those around me to do the same.

'Neart na Gaoithe' is what my Mainstream renewable power company christened a 105-square-kilometre stretch of water in the outer Firth of Forth. The name – from the Gaelic shared by the people of Ireland and Scotland – loosely translates as 'power of the wind'. Located about 15 kilometres from the shore, Neart na Gaoithe was one of 10 potential sites offered by Britain's Crown Estate in 2008 for development of offshore wind farms. Ascot racecourse and most of London's Regent Street are just a small part of the £12 billion portfolio of land and developments owned by the Crown Estate, an independent business created by a 1961 Act of Parliament. Some of the property it owns can be traced back to an 11th-century king of England, Edward the Confessor. The Crown Estate controls the rights to the seabed around Britain, so if you want to use it for commercial purposes – take rock, stone or pebbles for construction, say, or develop a wind farm – they are the people who give you the licence to do it.

Andy Kinsella, who headed our offshore team and led the Neart na Gaoithe project, joined me in May 2008, just about the time the Crown Estate first put out the offer on the Scottish offshore sites.

Early in 2009 we were selected as the preferred bidder for Neart, which meant we had convinced the Crown Estate of our ability to develop a 450MW wind farm on the site, generating enough power for about 325,000 homes, which would be equivalent to a city the size of Edinburgh. Although Mainstream was ostensibly a start-up, the entire offshore team of my previous company, Airtricity, had come on board with me when it was sold to SSE at the beginning of 2008. We had a highly successful track record in developing offshore wind farms – including what was at the time the world's biggest, the 650MW Greater Gabbard off England's Suffolk coast, in a joint venture with Texas company Fluor.

The calibre of my offshore team was evident right from the start. They narrowed down the choice of the 10 sites on offer, off the west and east coasts of Scotland. It was as if they had a crystal ball because the problems they predicted when ruling out half a dozen of them came to pass. Out of those 10 sites, just two progressed all the way to having wind farms built on them and one of those was ours.

Our elimination of unsuitable sites was down to experience and common sense. Two of the team, Cameron Smith and Cathryn Hooper, spent a day sitting on the cliffs at Fife Ness, a headland looking out over the Firth of Forth, where there were four sites. One was called Belrock, which is at the northern end, and they were watching RAF planes coming into the then RAF Leuchars station.

'There's no point in taking that site – too many military issues,' they reported back. Three years later, SSE went for that site and won it. Another three years on, after spending probably between £10–15 million, they walked away from it because they couldn't get past the military radar issues.

Three of the sites were in the Solway Firth on the other side of the country. Again, the team advised against going after those sites, saying they wouldn't get through the environmental impact assessment because the area was too sensitive. From their work on the ground, they believed there would be strong resistance among the local communities. Danish energy company Dong (now Ørsted), German utilities company RWE, and SSE each won a site there. Three years later, all three projects were rejected on environmental grounds. Two more sites were located further off the mainland, in the islands of western Scotland, and the team reckoned we would be barking mad to pursue these. That left the three in the Firth of Forth and we got one of them. A winning bid is not about money, it's a capability statement; you're proving your credentials to bring the project to fruition.

Before you can apply for permission to build any UK offshore wind farm, you have to do two years of bird surveys, covering two full cycles of nesting, breeding and fledging, as part of the environmental impact assessment. You also conduct surveys of fish, marine mammals such as dolphins, and the benthos – the organisms that live in and on the bottom of the ocean floor.

For business feasibility, a metocean campaign gathers a huge amount of data on the expanse of sea in question. For any proposed wind farm, you want to know the wind patterns, in terms of speed, direction, variability and turbulence, but for an offshore project the cost of establishing this is many multiples of carrying out the same exercise on land. For example, on the Hornsea One project, the met mast for measuring the wind speed cost £10 million. Onshore, the equivalent cost would have been about £100,000.

For Neart, where the sea had an average depth of 47 metres, the cheapest quote for a met mast was £18 million. That was a huge financial risk at an early stage of the project. By nature I am an innovator, always looking forward to the new possibilities of rapidly evolving technology. From my time in the 1980s–90s as managing director of BNM, and then with my own companies Airtricity and Mainstream, I have always been very comfortable with disruptive change. When we were embarking on Neart's metocean campaign, relatively new technology, called LiDAR, was using laser beams for measuring wind on land, and we knew there was a group trying to finalise an offshore version. They were experimenting with floating LiDAR out at sea, at a fraction of the cost of erecting a fixed mast. We were one of the early adopters of this technology and spent £2–2.5 million on it for our metocean campaign at Neart; the cost to us was further reduced by a grant of about £500,000 because it was a new technology. Thinking outside the box resulted in a huge saving for us.

No bank will finance a project like this until you have accumulated at least two years' wind data, but while you're doing that you want to progress on other fronts. The environmental impact assessment, involving the minimum of two years for the birds, has to be completed to get planning permission. While we didn't need to conduct our geo-tech campaign to investigate the seabed before getting consent, we wanted to complete as many strands of preparatory work in parallel as possible, to shorten the development time frame. With the geo-tech costing up to £17 million, investing so much in a venture that might not get the final go-ahead was a risk. However, our aim was to get it consented, with the metocean and geo-tech campaigns completed to inform a detailed and costed plan on how to build the wind farm. In addition, a grid connection had to be organised. This involved identifying and selecting a suitable local substation. Way leaves have to be organised on land and the path from the offshore wind farm has to be surveyed for suitability. Only then, with all these ducks in a row, would it be a saleable proposition.

As with any planning permission, local residents and businesses can object. There are obligations to consult with local communities but wherever Mainstream goes, we always put a lot of time and effort into winning hearts and minds. We had roadshows and booked community halls, giving out as much information as we could to fishermen, business people, local residents, politicians, charities and environmental groups, with people there to answer questions. An indication of our success at this in respect to Neart was that we got about 33 of what are called 'specific representations' lodged against our planning permission – these are not objections to the overall plan but to a particular aspect. Another big utility had more than 890 specific representations lodged against one of its offshore projects in the Irish Sea.

The guidelines for obtaining consent in Scotland differ from those of England and Wales, but it was supposed to be processed within nine months of application. That meant the decision on Neart should have been made by early 2013. However, not only was the application system struggling to perform as it should, wider political issues were also having an impact.

While our Neart development team was hard at work preparing the project's application for offshore and onshore consent, Scottish ministers remained bullish in their support for offshore wind. The UK government was rowing away from their backing for renewable energy at the same time that the Scottish government was pushing forward – to the displeasure of a certain future POTUS. First Minister Alex Salmond received a series of increasingly angry letters from billionaire Donald Trump, demanding that he cease cheerleading for offshore wind. Referring to wind farms as 'monsters', Trump suggested that Salmond 'let them ruin the coastline of Sweden first'; he also declared that 'wind power doesn't work', and warned him that 'your economy will become a third world wasteland that investors will avoid'.[22] Trump, who bought the Menie estate north of Aberdeen in 2006 and developed it as a golf resort, tried to prevent the building of 11 turbines about three

22   *The Guardian*, 21 December 2016.

kilometres offshore from the course. Trump accused Salmond – his one-time ally in getting planning permission for the Aberdeen resort – of being biased in favour of the wind farm project and skewing the approval process. Despite losing at every stage in the Scottish courts, Trump brought the challenge to the UK Supreme Court, where he also lost.[23]

As the months dragged on after the decision on consent for Neart was due, the project was joined in the planning queue by four others, further delaying the process. Our offshore leader, Andy Kinsella, was up and down to Scotland from the London office, lobbying civil servants and politicians, including Salmond, Nicola Sturgeon, Fergus Ewing and John Swinney, to try to get the application through the bureaucracy in which it seemed trapped. Andy remembers going to see Ewing and Swinney the day the Scottish Parliament was breaking up in preparation for the Scottish Independence Referendum, which was to be held on Thursday, 18 September 2014. It was apparent that the Royal Society for the Protection of Birds (RSPB) had been making civil servants and politicians fully aware of its opposition to all the wind farms proposed for the Firth of Forth.

The RSPB is the largest nature conservation charity in the UK, with more than one million members. MemberWise's top 100 of the UK's largest membership bodies has put the RSPB (with 1.1 million members) in eighth place on a list topped by the National Union of Students (7 million), the Trades Union Congress (5.6 million) and the National Trust (4 million).[24] Its Scottish membership was around 100,000 – a sizeable body of voters – and ministers were undoubtedly aware of its influence.

Andy was told that we would get our consent after the referendum. Sure enough, it came through four weeks after 55.3% of the Scottish people voted against independence.

---

23   *The Guardian*, 8 October 2015.
24   https://memberwise.org.uk/influence100/

The RSPB has opposed every UK offshore wind farm and th0se in the Firth of Forth were to be no exception. However, it didn't help that the Scottish government had lumped our application in with three other applications for planning permission that had been made much later than ours. Overall the ministers gave consent for wind farms with a combined output of 2,500MW and we had sought just 450MW. They must have known they were flying in the face of the RSPB who were campaigning hard about the cumulative impact. Sure enough, in May 2015 the charity sought a judicial review of the ministers' decision. They argued, in a case presided over by Lord Stewart in the Outer Court of Session, that the farms put birds such as the puffin, the gannet and kittiwake at risk.

You would think if the RSPB really cared about birds, they would be more concerned about global warming. We should be on the same side. We are committed to building new energy systems that will make a material contribution to combatting climate change, which has already had a far more detrimental effect on Britain's seabirds than the erection of turbines ever will.

For example, puffin colonies in the Northern Isles of Scotland have been devastated by the rising temperature of the water in their traditional feeding grounds. As the sea became warmer, sand eels, on which puffins feed, moved further out. This meant puffins had to travel greater distances for their dinner and to bring eels back to their chicks. The 'calories in, calories out' equation became fatally unbalanced. One puffin monitored by the RSPB was found to have flown more than 248 miles in order to find food – 10 times further than it had previously been thought they were flying.[25]

Figures for the bird population of Shetland show that while there were 33,000 puffins in the spring of 2000, the number had dropped to just 570 by 2017. Shetland's kittiwake population fell from more than 55,000 in 1981 to just 5,000 in 2011. In comparison, wind

---

25 https://www.scotsman.com, 3 June 2018.

farms have only a minuscule effect on birds. Take the gannet population in the Firth of Forth, which is between 25,000 and 30,000. Not only is it self-sustaining, it's probably overcrowded. Research had shown that the worst-case scenario of the impact of our Neart wind farm was that 130 gannets a year would be killed. There was no way it was going to decimate bird populations, as was being claimed. Birds are not stupid – they see the turbines. Yes, they can get distracted when evading a bird of prey or focusing on a source of food below to the extent that they don't look where they're going. However, collisions are very much the exception.

Scottish guidelines indicated that the judicial review requested by the RSPB should have taken about three months. Thirteen months later we were still waiting for a decision.

Meanwhile, needing a potential buyer for the power to be generated by Neart, we prepared our bid for what is called a contract for difference (CFD). The UK government-owned Low Carbon Contract Company (LCCC) enters agreements with sustainable energy producers to purchase power. The first CFDs, aimed at kickstarting the renewables industry, were given out in 2014 at a price of £140 per megawatt hour. Our bid for Neart sought a price of just £114.39 per megawatt hour; we were awarded the contract on 26 March 2015. While the LCCC had to accept our bid as the lowest, they were sceptical, as were industry competitors, that the wind farm would ever be built, believing we had pitched too low. It was a massive achievement for a small Irish start-up company to win the bid, and it illustrates the sort of disruptive change we were bringing to the industry.

Once the CFD was agreed, it gave us an inflation-linked price for the electricity that Neart would produce over its first 15 years of operation. This guaranteed revenue stream makes the wind farm a viable investment project and we had a year to get the finance into place to build it. However, because the question of consent was still before the courts as the judicial review dragged on, we couldn't reach the required 12-month milestone, which could be met in either of two ways. One was to have spent a fixed percentage of the development costs; the other was to achieve financial closure for the project. Andy was over and back to the LCCC, explaining that we could not secure financial backing for Neart until the court action over consent was completed. In entering arbitration with the LCCC to extend the deadlines, we argued *force majeure*, as the judicial proceedings were out of our hands.

On 29 March 2016, 12 months and three days after awarding us the CFD, representatives of the LCCC, without warning, walked into our head office in Sandyford, south Dublin. They handed the receptionist a letter terminating our CFD, citing Mainstream's inability to meet its obligations under the contract. We hadn't reached financial closure, nor had we spent the £83 million required within the year, having expended less than £50 million at that stage. A couple of months later, in answer to a parliamentary question, the then UK energy minister, Andrea Leadsom, announced publicly that Neart's CFD had been cancelled. It seemed to many that the project was dead in the water. The prognosis became even bleaker when, on 18 July 2016, Lord Stewart issued his opinion on the RSPB's petition for judicial review. The charity had four parts to their case and Lord Stewart found in its favour on every single one. He ruled that the Scottish Ministers had failed to give proper consideration to the area's being a haven for certain species of seabirds. He also found that the government had failed to consult properly with interested parties about the environmental impact of the wind farms and had acted unlawfully by taking into account 'unconsulted information' when decisions on the consents were made.[26]

26   https://www.bbc.com/news/uk-scotland-39934095

We got to see the ruling the day before it was made public and Andy, who happened to be in our Dublin office that day, got the Neart team to dial in from London and Scotland for a conference call so that he could deliver the devastating news. In the pervading air of gloom, our then head of electrical engineering John O'Reilly, who had known Andy since 1986, tried to rally his colleagues: 'Don't worry about this – Andy always has a plan B'. it was like being in a long dark tunnel, without a light at either end. However, I was determined that this ship was not sinking.

CHAPTER 11

Outgreening the Bird People

To save Neart, Mainstream had to come out fighting on two fronts. While other companies might have cut their losses in that situation, my attitude was that you spend more money because you believe in it. As both CEO and chief shareholder at Mainstream, I was in a position of considerable power in that regard.

In the efforts to get our CFD reinstated, we had invoked dispute procedures with the LCCC over termination of the contract. This went to an arbitration tribunal in London and we spared no expense to hire Laurence Rabinowitz QC, who had a track record of winning billion-pound cases and was one of the best silks at the English Commercial Bar, to lead our challenge.

However, without consent, we had no prospect of regaining our power purchase agreement. So, were the Scottish ministers going to appeal Lord Stewart's judgment against them in favour of the RSPB?

Andy started making representations to the new Scottish minister for energy, Paul Wheelhouse, to lodge an appeal. The development companies for the other two sites and the Scottish government were also caught up in this. Andy was told that the QC from whom the government wanted advice was in Spain and would be back in two weeks. The permissible time frame of 21 days for lodging an appeal to the Inner Court of Session was ticking away. Eventually the QC advised the Scottish government that he didn't believe they could win the case. While he thought they might get the judgment reversed on one of the four points, he couldn't see them clawing back all four. On foot of that advice, the Scottish government informed us it wouldn't be appealing and instead would restart the consent process that Lord Stewart had ruled was flawed.

At Mainstream, now in full Plan B mode, we immediately put it up to the government by saying we would bring a challenge to Lord Stewart's opinion to the Inner House of the Court of Session ourselves. Knowing that they couldn't go ahead with reconsenting the sites if we had a case before the courts, the Scottish government came back within a week to say they'd go with us on the appeal, which would be lodged in the name of the 'Scottish Ministers and Others'.

The arbitration tribunal hearing our dispute with the LCCC over our power purchase contract met in January 2017. Just two months later it announced that it had found in Mainstream's favour and the CFD deal was deemed to be still in place. After that legal victory in London, we then had to await the result of the court case in Scotland, to see if we could get Neart back on track.

Three judges of the Inner Court of Session, presided over by Scotland's most senior judge, Lord Carloway, heard the appeal against Lord Stewart's ruling. The time frame guideline for a ruling was three months and in this case the judges delivered. On 16 May 2017, Lord Carloway, who was sitting with judges Lord Menzies and Lord Brodie, issued a ruling upholding the appeal. The written judgment was damning of Lord Stewart's handling of the case, stating that he had greatly exceeded the work he was supposed to do. They restated the law of judicial review, pointing out that 'it is not the role of the Court to test the ecological or planning judgements made in the course of the decision-making process'.

They continued: 'Despite paying lip service to the correct legal test for judicial review, the Lord Ordinary has strayed well beyond the limits of testing the legality of the process and has turned himself into the decision-maker following what appears to have been treated as an appeal against the respondents' decisions on the facts. He has acted, almost as if he were the reporter at such an inquiry, as a finder of fact on matters of scientific fact and methodology which, whatever the judge's own particular skills may be, are not within the proper province of a court of review.'[27]

At every stage we had worked closely and patiently with our environmental partners to assess and mitigate the potential impact of Neart on marine wildlife. The Inner Court of Session judges recognised that in their decision.

Of course, the RSPB has a duty to its members to act to protect the UK's bird populations and we have had a constructive relationship with them for many years. What was disappointing was that in order to justify the judicial review, they sought to overstate dramatically the potential impact of wind farms on bird life in the Forth and Tay estuaries. Their suggestion that thousands of gannets could be harmed was so far from reality that it undermined our ability to work together to find common solutions to minimise the effects of climate change on marine wildlife. What's more, they knew that advances in turbine technology since the project was first conceived in 2009 had enabled us to redesign the site with about half the number of proposed turbines, situated about a kilometre apart, so providing much wider corridors for bird transit between them.

The sort of people that the RSPB attracts is illustrated by a letter from Glasgow that Andy Kinsella received at our Dublin office. It included newspaper clippings of interviews he had given to the Scottish media, with the comment: 'Your behaviour is akin to AH in 1936.' The letter was signed by an RSPB member, giving full name and address and membership number, and it was copied to RSPB Scotland's HQ. Kinsella wrote to RSPB regional director Anne McCall, pointing out that he couldn't think of anything

27 http://www.scotland-judiciary.org.uk/9/1784/
    RSPB-v-The-Scottish-Ministers-And-Others

much worse than being compared to Adolf Hitler. He received no reply, and only when he wrote again did he get the response that that they had more than a million members and they couldn't be responsible for all of them. Andy was shocked at their attitude and the fact that he needed to write back again, pointing out that while he knew they had more than a million members, we were only talking about one here and that person was clearly identified by name and membership number. Eventually Andy got the assurance that the individual had been spoken to and there would be no repeat of the behaviour. Surely a truly ethical organisation would have taken a member to task as soon as it became aware of such an abusive letter being sent in its name?

Consent for Neart was back on, thanks to the appeals court judges. However, despite suffering this heavy loss, the RSPB wouldn't let the matter rest. They went back to the Inner Court of Session to seek leave to appeal this latest ruling – although they failed to get it there, they appealed it anyway. They were entitled to go directly to the UK Supreme Court for permission to appeal, which they did successfully, further delaying the project.

As well as the advances in turbine technology, there had also been increased understanding of how seabirds behaved around wind farms. The Offshore Renewables Joint Industry Programme (ORJIP) Bird Collision Avoidance Study, conducted over two years at the 100-turbine Thanet wind farm off the Kent coast, showed how five targeted species of seabirds, including the Northern Gannet, the Black-legged Kittiwake and various gulls, took avoidance measures when flying in the vicinity. 'These behaviours significantly reduce the risk of those seabird species colliding with rotating turbine blades than would otherwise be the case if there was no change in behaviour', it noted.[28] Before this collection of real-life data, bird collision risk modelling had been predicated

28   9.1.3 ORJIP Bird Collision Avoidance Study.

on no avoidance being taken and then 'corrected' to take account of some evasion and other uncertainties. 'The key finding of this study, therefore, is that there is very strong, empirical evidence to assume very high avoidance of offshore wind turbines by the target seabird species investigated. This provides a compelling basis for using higher avoidance rates, for these species, than are currently advised for use in collision risk assessment in the UK', the authors concluded.[29] Although the final report was not published until April 2018, the RSPB were aware of the data at that stage, which made their strident reaction to the court decision so puzzling.

After the RSPB announced that it would seek leave to appeal the decision to the Supreme Court in London, Mainstream and businesses affected by the stalling of Neart launched a public relations offensive. The idea of a campaigning coalition to pressurise the RSPB to drop its continuing legal action arose out of a dinner Andy had with five managing directors of the companies who would do the biggest business with Neart if it went ahead. These were influential industry leaders, some of whom were also on government task forces, and they were able to bring the campaign down to the grassroots.

We knew we couldn't engage with the RSPB in the public arena about killing birds as we would never win that sort of emotive argument in their area of expertise. So instead, the Neart na Gaoithe Offshore Wind Farm Coalition focused its message on the killing of jobs and communities if the wind farm did not go ahead. A series of print advertisements was endorsed by more and more companies, until we couldn't shrink the logos of more than 70 of them small enough to fit them into a page. Mainstream paid for a dedicated website and for the marketing and got everybody riled up. The coalition is still going today, as a lobbying group for offshore wind to keep the jobs and investment in Scotland.

29   9.1.14 ORJIP Bird Collision Avoidance Study.

In November 2017, the RSPB's leave to appeal was denied, in a one-line judgment from the UK Supreme Court. The day that judgment was issued, Andy was working in the Mainstream office in the business district of Santiago in Chile. At about 8.30am local time, as he was walking towards the office with our CFO, Mary Quaney, he looked at his phone and saw a couple of missed calls from Neart project director Aidan Guinan. Then a text came in saying simply 'we have won – leave for appeal rejected'. As he shared the news with Mary and they were hugging each other on the street in jubilation, he reckons people walking by probably thought he had just proposed to her. At last, with both the power purchase agreement and consent cemented in, we could put the ready-to-build Neart wind farm up for sale.

The twist in the tale is that, ultimately, the RSPB did us a huge favour. During the years they spent trying to derail the project, the renewable energy industry was heading for what I call its 'iPhone moment'.

When Apple released the first iPhone in June 2007, it was hailed as an interesting product and seen as a challenge to the existing mobile phone market, but few predicted the dramatic change that it ushered in. The smartphone is now ubiquitous, and it has created entirely new companies and services that didn't exist before its launch. By the end of 2017, renewable energy had reached that same launch point and I could confidently forecast that, within the next decade, it too would have a transformative effect on the electricity market across the world. Renewable energy is essentially a technology business – with rapid change and innovation delivering ever-decreasing prices, and constant improvement in performance.

In 2016 Mainstream had done a provisional deal to sell Neart to a consortium that consisted of Siemens, InterGen (US) and two finance groups – the Marguerite Fund and Infracapital. That sale would have brought in around €110–120 million, but we never reached financial closure because Neart was still caught up in the court action over consent. The consortium was not prepared to take the risk that planning permission could be achieved.

Just two years later, in early 2018, after we had cleared the last legal hurdle, Neart na Gaoithe was sold to the French utilities giant Électricité de France (EDF) for €650 million – giving us a massive return on the €48 million we had spent on the site. While Neart's locked-in CFD was £114, the winning bid in the UK's next round of CFDs was almost exactly half, just £57.50, due to the tumbling costs within the renewable energy industry. This meant we were selling a wind-farm project that would get double the price for its power compared to those coming after it.

The sale of Neart enabled us to clear all debt and buy out Marubeni and Barclays who owned 25% of the business. We, namely myself with a 57% stake, management, staff and directors with 8%, and private investors with 35% – were left in total control of the business, with no debt and €400 million in cash. It consolidated our position as the leading independent developer of some of the most significant and complex wind and solar projects across Europe, South America, Africa and Asia. That's no mean feat for a Plan B.

If one broadens the debate on the role of NGOs and peripheral green parties in the world's struggle to contain and limit climate change, a strange and equivocal picture emerges. Bird populations are heavily dependent on food sources, and it was a shortage of food that virtually eliminated the puffin population of St Kilda. There was a shortage because the sea had heated up. Whatever the sand eels fed on moved north and the sand eels followed them. The 32,000 puffins that died did so as a direct result of global warming. One would have thought that the RSPB would strongly support their fellow environmentalists who wanted to create a better climate for biodiversity.

CHAPTER 12

Company Culture and Values

When Airtricity was on occasion referred to in the media as 'the Ryanair of renewable energy' it was shorthand for a financially successful Irish company proving itself internationally.

The similarities ended there. Michael O'Leary went into an industry in which the average profit had been less than zero since the Wright brothers first flew. He turned Ryanair into a highly profitable global leader. Our industry is very different, so the style used to manage has to be different as well. Ryanair is low cost. Every aspect of the business, from purchasing aeroplanes to not selling peanuts to selling lottery tickets is managed to create profits.

My style of management has to be different, because we are an emerging industry, driven by a need to decarbonise and to spend a great deal of management time interacting with policy-makers and politicians. Even at this late stage in the evolution of the renewables industry there are still big technology, integration, electricity storage and connectivity issues to be solved. All of these are happening in a policy context that was designed for a different energy set-up. This, still current, energy context is all about fossil fuels. Analyst Ian Morris says, 'When we look at the entire planet across the last twenty thousand years, I argue, we see three broadly successive systems of human values. Each is associated with a particular way of organizing society, and each form of organization is dictated by a particular way of capturing energy from the world around us.'[30] Twenty thousand years is a proper time frame.

Management creates the culture of a company. Culture is something that builds up over time and answers the question 'How do we do things around here?' A major expression of the culture is the values that the company espouses. With Airtricity, and then Mainstream, I was building companies from scratch, so I could inculcate them with my management values from the outset.

Before that, as when I went into BNM, I had to find a way to change a very bureaucratic, dysfunctional organisation. It was there I learned how to establish and apply values, which played a part in turning the company around.

In BNM there had been a huge gulf between the management and the workers. Former CEOs had not met with staff representatives. I saw this as a lack of respect for the majority of the people in the company. Respect is a two-way street. If you disrespect people, then they disrespect you. If, on the other hand, you show respect, then it's reciprocated.

I believe I earned the respect of the workers through my extensive consultations at all the production centres. However, winning over the upper and middle management layers of staff was more difficult because they were the principal beneficiaries of the old system. They knew change was needed but they were fearful about what this would mean for them personally. Their reactions ranged from outright opposition, to passive aggression, to acceptance.

It was at this point I was introduced to the concept of values by the late Sean Brophy, a psychologist working as a corporate consultant. He introduced me to four constructs by which I could understand my fellow managers. The first was a test that could be undertaken to determine if one was 'on purpose' or not; the second

30   Ian Morris, *Foragers, Farmers and Fossil Fuels: How Humans Evolve*, Princeton, NJ: Princeton University Press, 2017.

tested whether you were oriented towards the future, present or past; the third concerned the 'Mind Maker 6 construct', which I will come back to later, and the fourth and most significant one was the importance of values.

Values can unify a management team in their view of what is good and what is not. I hoped that by agreeing on a long-term 'good' for BNM, short-term disagreements could be circumvented. This worked only partially because the values the company had espoused up to then were deeply ingrained.

Another reason why an agreed set of values did not have the effect they were to have at Airtricity or Mainstream was the attitude of the owner, as represented by the Civil Service. From the outset the Civil Service had opposed many of the changes that I needed to make. Some of the old management spent a good proportion of their time persuading various civil servants that my programme was wrong. At one stage an instruction came from the Civil Service that I was to stop recruitment of senior management to replace the people I had let go.

Even a member of the staff I had recruited had been busy, for personal advancement, telling the Civil Service that the company would have changed itself and that he would be a much better, safer pair of hands from there on. This person was entirely risk averse, and as such was closely aligned with the philosophy and modus operandi of the Civil Service.

However, the majority of the staff believed in the values I was promoting, those of entrepreneurship, customer focus, safety and, most of all, innovation. The Employee Enterprise Scheme, the new bio-filter products, Puraflo and Biophore, the haku system, the Clonmacnoise and West Offaly Railway, the bog wood sculptures, and the replacement of all four old, inefficient peat-fired power stations with three new ones using fluidised bed boilers, were instances of where innovation was to contribute towards the long-term survival of the company.

The later businesses I set up myself are development companies, working with communities all over the world. When you do development you always have an impact on communities because you are changing the physical environment in which people live and work. Carefully considered values informed a set of rules that evolved at Airtricity and then Mainstream as to how to do development business.

This culminated in the 'Mainstream Global Development Standard'. It is firmly rooted in community engagement but includes the engineering activities that are needed to build a wind farm or a solar PV system. For a renewable energy plant to be able to attract financing there need to be accurate measurements of wind speed, usually over two years. In the case of solar the intensity of radiation at the proposed site is measured.

We embed our values in the methods used to do development everywhere. They have been tested and proven to work in diverse cultures, in various countries on the continents of Europe, North America, South America, Africa and Asia. The local culture always dictates what has to be done to achieve planning permission. The need to have respect for the communities in which you work is obvious – coming in and riding roughshod over local sensibilities is going to generate opposition. Our approach has always been to give communities loads of information – what we are going to do, and how it is going to affect them and their environment.

In every situation, the standards of behaviour that you live by come into play. Some people will adopt the position of 'getting by' and maybe ignoring rules; others will work strictly according to rules; a few, like us, will go above and beyond what the rules require in the belief that the longest way around is the shortest way home. You don't lie. When you do a deal with somebody you don't cheat them. It is very hard to do business in some parts of the world without cheating, that is without paying out in brown paper parcels, particularly when you are building infrastructure that is going to affect local communities and negotiating with local big-wigs who have to give the say-so. We don't do that and, if we did, it would turn us into our own worst enemy. If once you get the reputation for corruption, you're sunk. I wouldn't do it anyway because I don't think it is the appropriate way to do business.

The fundamental value we have is respect. We always see ourselves as being around for the long term so we are not transaction based. That means our approach is not just to do a deal and walk away, regardless of the reputation we might leave behind. We see ourselves doing business in the community, and that community and culture will be a reference for any other future development that we do there or, indeed, anywhere else. I have always believed in building a profound brand, whether it was BNM, Airtricity, Mainstream or wherever.

I wrote about my respect for the environment in my introduction. Respect is an all-embracing value. It is like the base of a triangle, insofar as it is the foundation of all the other values.

If there is a second founding value it is innovation. Entrepreneurship, teamwork, sustainability and safety are the other values. All profitable enterprises make use of the profound value of innovation. When you consider the great leaders in history, many were military men who were outstanding innovators as well.

You have to innovate. If you look at all the changes that have come about in the world of business, it's all about innovation: doing things differently, changing the rules of engagement and maybe sometimes copying what a good competitor does or borrowing their break-throughs. I found that by changing everything you add value to your shareholders who invested in you. It is also more exciting for staff.

While respect and innovation are two kinds of fundamental value, my companies also prioritise entrepreneurship as a value. A lot of people might argue that entrepreneurship and innovation are one and the same, but while it is possible to be an entrepreneur without innovating, I think everybody should strive to have some unique source of competitive advantage. Entrepreneurship is about adding the necessary value of capital and other resources to innovative ideas. You can innovate and add cost, but just adding cost is not much use to anybody without a value-adding end goal in sight. However, when you add entrepreneurship into your value system, then you are talking about investing and organising to allocate resources, money and people. Entrepreneurship brings the connectivity that you need for business to evolve.

An innovative company needs an entrepreneurial board, which is capable of reaching decisions quickly. I believe in setting up a board and company in a way that minimises bureaucracy. I want to have very clear lines of communication between the board and the company so that there are no big delays if something needs timely intervention. It's why the value of entrepreneurship matters and is important in the whole set-up of the company.

Mainstream values itself as a green company that does not do anything other than renewable energy, which is the future. It is difficult to do the future, because most people live in the present; a significant section of humanity lives in the past – although they are generally not to be found in business. Driving down the road with your eyes only on the rear-view mirror guarantees that you will crash.

At Mainstream we are locked on to the future by virtue of our focus on green energy and nothing else. We have had opportunities to do non-green things, to invest in gas-fired plant or coal-fired plant, for instance, or even to put some money into nuclear research, but we have done none of that because we are a green company.

It's tough, because a lot of the things you are trying to do will not have been done before. Everybody likes to point out that renewables are a variable source of supply and can't provide customers with electricity that can be counted on. How do you cope with that?

If we had become fixated on the idea of having to have a constant source of supply, we wouldn't have done what we have done. Instead we did a lot of analysis of how to serve the customer with a variable source of supply. The banking of power, as we did in Airtricity, was a strategy that worked well in coping with the variability of wind. Of course it needed a supportive regulatory regime, and that is what we created when we intervened in the formulation of the Electricity Regulation Act of 1999. We knew renewable energy was the right thing to do, so it was a matter of forging ahead, with the confidence that we would figure out how to cope with issues as we went along and learn by doing.

When entrepreneurship is combined with innovation, it's impossible to predict all the outcomes. They are unforeseen because nobody has done it before and sometimes no amount of analysis will allow you to predict what will actually happen. Working with partial amounts of information, you take the leap anyway.

When we were setting up Airtricity we weren't able to get any government contracts because they didn't really want any wind energy in the system, and the ESB certainly didn't want any renewable energy. So we went out and got our own customers. We didn't know whether we were going to be able to get sufficient funding from banks to build plant but, ultimately, we did, because we were seen to be doing the right thing. The banks gave us only 56% senior debt for our first plant at Culliagh, but when they saw we had more customers and the rules of the system had been changed, allowing us to meet our customer demand from green sources, then we had 65% debt for the second year and by the third year we had 75% debt.

We had invented a new way of doing things. Of course, it wasn't perfect in the beginning, but what makes an entrepreneur is knowing you may not get it all right the first time. However, you learn so much from having done it, particularly in comparison to those who didn't do it. You know you will do it much better the second time around, and the third time around you will be verging on perfection.

That is the mindset of the entrepreneur. That is the mindset I have taken into everything I have done, in every business. Even in BNM, where enterprise might once have seemed like an alien concept, I brought entrepreneurship into the equation through the switch to payment according to productivity, rather than time worked.

The value of teamwork was taken on board in Mainstream. We wanted to create a company in which there were centres of excellence. We could not afford to replicate every skill in every location. Differing skill sets, such as energy estimation, corporate finance, offshore expertise, information technology, purchasing, insurance etc., are needed to run the business. I wanted to create a company where any member of staff in any location could phone or email a colleague and be guaranteed that they would address the issue. As we had not conceived Airtricity as an international company the value of teamwork didn't need to be included. In Mainstream it was necessary, and I consider it has worked well.

Our values resemble a triangle. Respect is the founding value and is at the base of the triangle. The other values – innovation, green, entrepreneurship, teamwork – sit on top of respect. At the apex of the triangle is the value of safety.

As I studied the histories of fatalities in power station construction, I realised that safety was a management function. The more attention that was given to safety the fewer workplace injuries and deaths there were. All meetings within Airtricity or Mainstream at management or at board level begin with a review of safety. Not only do we measure lost time incidents, but near misses and observations as well. We discovered that most accidents in the company are due to transport. Only by constant monitoring, including safety audits and safety walks, can the behaviour of working staff be adjusted. I remember the great pride I felt when we had a million man hours of construction on Jeffreys Bay in South Africa without a single lost-time incident. This was particularly pleasing as many of the workers had never worked in an industrial set-up before, and many had been picked up along the side of the road in a nearby town. It isn't good enough to have values written on posters and hanging from walls. To make them stick we award a prize to staff at all our general company meetings. There are six, maybe eight general company meetings each year. We choose a 'person of the moment' or, indeed, 'a team of the moment', the living embodiment of one of the company values.

Members of a company, or of any team, have deep ethical needs. The younger they are the greater their need to feel that they are doing the right thing, but staff of any age feel this way. I have noticed how successful managers and coaches go beyond the immediate requirements of the job and find ways to reach deeper levels of motivation for the group they lead. Pat Lamb was the coach of the Connacht team, which achieved huge success. The culmination of his achievement was winning the Pro12 rugby championship. Connacht beat one of the great teams of world rugby, Leinster, in the final in Edinburgh in 2016. There are perhaps 20 times as many rugby players in Leinster as there are in Connacht. I heard Pat explain how he brought the team to meet with communities in the West of Ireland. He instilled in them the feeling that they weren't just playing for themselves. They carried the hopes and dreams of every Connacht schoolboy and community.

I also had the wonderful experience of hearing Clive Woodward describe how he led the successful UK Olympic team of 2012. He explained how difficult it was to bring a feeling of teamship to 541 athletes from 26 different sports, many of whom had never met or perhaps even heard of one another before the Games. His whole approach centred around values. He talked about teams and how teams celebrated one another's success. He told how, at the previous Olympics in Beijing, he had been standing in a queue behind a huge figure at 2.30 one morning. It was only when Rafael Nadal collected his six Big Macs and chips that Clive realised who he was. Here was this great athlete collecting food for fellow athletes. It was by recalling such tales that he built a common bond between disparate members of the team. The UK team went on to exceed expectations and bring home a record haul of 65 medals.

CHAPTER 13

The Nature of Leadership

Loyalty seems to work best in politics. Unquestioning adherence to a single person is the meat and drink of political systems. In business it doesn't work like this. That might sound counter-intuitive, coming from a business leader, but I know that if it suits staff to be with you, they will be with you. However, people grow and evolve and seek new challenges, or life changes for them and their current working conditions no longer suit them and they move on. They are going to do their own thing, and rightly so.

Everybody is ambitious for themselves; if you don't look out for yourself how will anyone else look out for you? Loyalty is irrelevant, really, particularly with talented people; they will be loyal to their own concept of themselves and their future and the way they see life for themselves. Part of the maturing process is to realise that you are effectively the master of your own destiny.

However, holding on to trained staff can be important. It's why I have always tried to make working in my company a good experience for staff. Before Airtricity was sold, it was named in 2007 as 'The No.1 Best Company to Work For in Ireland' by the Great Place To Work Institute. It would always be my goal to achieve that.

I read a lot about companies that are difficult places in which to work. This is not because the work is hard or the hours are long. It is because the managers are not interested, or drive their staff in the wrong direction, or substitute ego enhancement for purposeful people management. So many companies are disastrous places to work in because all they see is the bottom line. Financial institutions are naked in their 'what's in it for me now' attitude, and never mind tomorrow. I've always thought it better to try and create a great company, built to deliver on an ennobling vision of a better society, in which all the employees see and understand their role in creating this better future. I once read a quote from Theodore Roosevelt which summed up much of what motivates people: 'Far and away the best prize that life has to offer is the chance to work hard at work worth doing.' It is up to the manager to create that vital link between the company vision and the employees' vision for themselves. A good part of motivation is about receiving praise and admiration from the significant people in their life, in particular their manager at work. It also helps to have a deep respect for one's workers. This will come through in the manager's body language and actions.

Contrary to the current business ideology of maximising shareholder value and aligning top managers' pay with owners' expectations, I have always thought that money is a great motivator until you have enough for all the normal necessities in life. After this it is a hygiene factor. I feel somewhat ashamed to be put in the same class as managers who earn many thousands of times what their lowest-paid employees earn.

Authenticity is a key to good leadership, walking the talk as they say. A great example is the Carthaginian general Hannibal Barca, most celebrated for his 218 BC crossing of the Alps into Italy with his troops and 38 African war elephants, to attack the Romans during the Second Punic War. That might be going back a bit, but I don't think as humans we have changed a great deal. Cultures have changed and technology has utterly altered daily living but we're still human beings, with basically the same DNA. I don't think our IQ has increased. Hannibal was an absolute genius who led an army of soldiers who had signed up as mercenaries but believed enough in him to forgo payment. They anticipated living off the fat of conquered lands. They followed him over the Pyrenees and all across southern France. Each step of the way they encountered hostile tribes. Their greatest logistic feat was to cross the Alps. Records showed that Hannibal brought his wife with him and that she perished while crossing the Alps, along with one of his children.

A master battle strategist, Hannibal led the Carthaginians to a series of battle victories, one of the greatest being at Lake Trasimene (the modern Trasimeno), where they defeated Roman legions led by Consul Gaius Flaminius. British military historian Sir Basil Liddell Hart (1895–1970) described it as 'the greatest ambush in history'.

Hannibal, who has been a big influence on me, won that battle by studying his enemies. All strategy is competitive, and Hannibal exhibited this skill consummately. He studied Flaminius and learned that he was an impulsive man. Hannibal made the consul think the Carthaginians were trying to bypass the Roman troops by turning his army in an unexpected direction in full view just before darkness fell. The following morning the Romans started to follow the Carthaginians, unaware Hannibal had split his army and had the cavalry hidden and waiting to ambush them. The Roman army was strung out between forested hills and Lake Trasimene. Their entire flank was exposed to Hannibal's cavalry, and a great slaughter ensued.

It was a strategy Hannibal was to deploy to even bloodier effect at the subsequent Battle of Cannae. His man management skills came to the fore. On the morning of the battle, as the forces drew up, a Carthaginian officer named Gisgo reportedly remarked to Hannibal that the size of the Roman army was astonishing. 'There is one thing, Gisgo, yet more astonishing,' Hannibal replied coolly, 'which you take no notice of.' He then explained, 'In all those great numbers before us, there is not one man called Gisgo,' provoking laughter that spread through the Carthaginian ranks. This was the laughter

Young Eddie in Monaghan, 1957

Eddie with brother Des and sister Mary

Photo taken by Pat Kenny, Newstalk, *when Eddie was running for President of SRC in 1968*

Rob, Hildegarde, Stewart, Lesley, Eddie at Lesley and Stewart's wedding, June 2012

At the helm in Dún Laoghaire Harbour

Business
& Finance

28TH JANUARY – 24TH FEBRUARY 2010
€4.98 INCLUDING VAT
STG£4.48/$7.27

Green Power
Eddie O'Connor on Mainstream's future
and how to get the economy moving

Read us online: www.businessandfinancetoday.com

Business & Finance, *28 January–24 February 2010*

In front of Bord na Móna Head office, 76 Lower Baggot Street

Business & Finance, *7 December–20 December 2007*

Irish Entrepreneur, *Volume 5, Issue 11, 2008*

Natural
CAPITAL

SUSTAINABILITY FINANCE,
INNOVATION & LEADERSHIP

EDDIE O'CONNOR
THE WIND WIZARD
The man at the
helm of the
world's most
successful
independent
renewable
energy
company
By Angela Madden

+

AIB SWITCHES ON
€1 BILLION IN
NEW LENDING
TO ENERGY SECTOR
By Kathleen Barrington

IRELAND: A NATION OF
4 MILLION FEEDING
400 MILLION
By Martha Kearns

GLEN DIMPLEX -
HOT STUFF WHEN IT COMES
TO ENERGY EFFICIENCY
By Mark Nicholls

VOLUME 1 / ISSUE 1 / DEC 2013 / JAN 2014

2013 – THE
€3 BILLION
YEAR FOR
IRELAND'S
GREEN
ASSET
MANAGERS

BLACKROCK
RENEWABLE
POWER
KLEINWORT
BENSON
INVESTORS
AMARENCO
GAELECTRIC
POWER CAPITAL
MAINSTREAM
RENEWABLE POWER
BNRG RENEWABLES

Visiting the coal mines in Australia in 1986

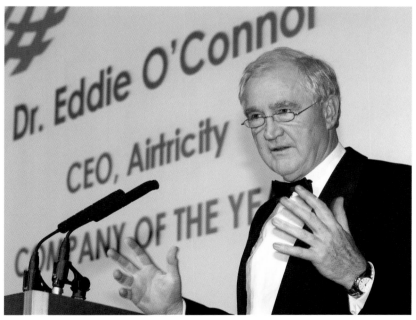

Company of the year, Airtricity 2007

Eddie with Hildegarde after receiving an honorary doctorate from the National University of Ireland, Maynooth, June 2011

Eddie with Professor Thomas Collins, former President of NUI, Maynooth, 2011

Eddie with Joanna Yarrow of IKEA and David Gascon of Vayu, August 2013.
The photo marked the purchase of the 7.6MW Carickeeny Wind Farm by IKEA

At Goldwind Wind Farm in Illinois circa 2014

EWEA (European Wind Energy Association) event in Barcelona, 2014

EWEA event in Barcelona, 2014

Ayitepa, Ghana, 2015

Ayitepa, Ghana, 2015

Eddie receiving the Preferred Developer 2015 award from Heather Sonn, South African Wind Energy Association (SAWEA), and South Africa's Minister for Energy, Tina Joemat-Petterson at the SAWEA Awards Ceremony, Cape Town, 2016

Akinwumi Adesina, President of the African Development Bank, meeting Eddie on 23 November 2016

Meeting with former President of Chile, Michelle Bachalet, June 2016

Meeting with Michelle Bachalet, June 2016

of pride. He could not have chosen a more dramatic way of saying 'We are better than them.' The subtlety of this comment, the location and timing of the remark have all the hallmarks of a carefully thought-out motivational bombshell. I would wager that Hannibal dreamt up this comment some time before. It had materialised somewhere in his imagination and he had waited for the right time to say it. Good battle strategy isn't enough to win. Each member of Hannibal's army believed he could outfight any Roman. Hannibal was right in the middle of his army when he fought and won the Battle of Cannae. More than 2,000 years later, his apparently simple remark to Gisgo inspired many of my dealings with staff. However, despite Hannibal's military prowess, it could be argued that his ultimate political strategy was wrong. He should never have been in Italy because Carthage could have carved out an empire in Africa and half of Spain and then traded peacefully with Rome. But Hannibal's father, Hamilcar Barca, brought him up with an intense dislike for Rome. It was preordained, if you like, that he would wage war on them. If he had had wiser counsel back in Carthage, they could have used him as a brilliant general, to carve out and defend a new realm.

The only way to defeat Hannibal was to copy him. That is what Publius Cornelius Scipio Africanus (Scipio) did, with support from the Numidian leader, Masinissa. The Romans lured Hannibal back to North Africa by starting an offensive there and were ultimately victorious at the Battle of Zama in Tunisia, in 202 BC, ending the Second Punic War.

As an authentic leader, there is nobody to compare with Hannibal. He never asked his troops to do anything he wasn't prepared to do himself – 'A leader leads by example, not by force.'[31] He clearly had a lot of diplomatic skills as he had a good relationship with the tribes in Northern Italy. He influenced military history right up to the Second World War.

31   Sun Tzu, *The Art of War*.

My learnings from Hannibal centre around his authenticity, his relationship with his men, his many military innovations and his success. I have often thought of what Hannibal did as the equivalent of a modern Canadian army invading the US. A bit fanciful, but it helped build the heroism of Hannibal in my mind.

There is huge emphasis on leadership now in the world of business. One of the principal things that any business leader has to have is a vision of where the company is going. All good leaders and managers seek to build a bridge between company goals and the individual workers' personal goals.

You have to have a vision and be able to turn that into a series of executable activities. As the Bible says, 'without a vision the people perish', an astute observation about the wellsprings of motivation of the human heart. At recent lectures to top business prospects at Harvard Business School it was pointed out to the class that more than half of them would quit working in their 40s, to do something that represented excitement and purpose for them. Aiming to achieve an increment of profit or a higher share price is no harm, but neither is it particularly motivational. If, however, a manager is able to build a link between a staff member's work output and winning the race to higher profit or share price increase, then that is a measurement of success for the staff member. It always helps if the staff share financially in the success. This is why we have always given staff share options, and annual bonuses related to performance.

Choice is increasing for young people who are entering the workforce. To attract the best it isn't sufficient to promise great rewards. Giving young people a noble vision to which they can anchor their careers is of equal importance. It is hard to find any young people who are global warming deniers. When the new CEO of BP, Kerryman Bernard Looney, has committed his company to carbon neutrality by 2050, you realise that two distinct forces are at work: young people are reluctant to work for a company that is destroying the atmosphere for humans, and investors are becoming increasingly reluctant to put hard-earned money to work with a fossil fuel company.

You plan – and you control according to plan, which involves lots of organisational structures. You must put people in doable jobs; they might stretch them considerably but they are still doable jobs and people should be stretched. I would concede that I could be accurately criticised for giving people too high a target at times. That is where learning comes in. Learning is such an important part of every business in every walk of life. Conditions, suppliers, competitors and technology all change rapidly. If you are playing with yesterday's tools, you are going to lose.

I spend a lot of time reading and listening – it comes easily to me because I assume the future is going to change and I want to know precisely how it is going to happen. It gives me immense pleasure to get this right, to live in the future. An awareness of that mixture of human, cultural and technological dynamics makes it possible to carve out a niche in that milieu and be successful by commercial standards, with big profits or a high share price or whatever commercial measure is most appropriate.

However, don't start with the measure: that is the end of the pipe and you can't start at the end. What are you doing, and where, when and why are you doing it? You have to be able to answer those questions; the more coherence and logic you bring to the answers, the better you will be able to lead people in that direction. When you address their inner fundamental being, their *raison d'être* for living, then they will go the extra mile. That's very important.

According to the Myers-Briggs psychology test I am highly intuitive. By definition this implies that I am not very sensitive. When I went into BNM, Brendan Halligan had a psychological assessment done on me that said I was missing some of my signals. It's true. I am sure I missed signals all the time but I do understand a little of how people are moved to do things – maybe imperfectly, but I try to understand that. I miss simple signals as I tend to operate at a high level.

I used to think it was because I was lazy that I delegated a lot. Now I don't think it is laziness; it is that I choose not to act at that level but instead to let people have their head, to let them own their own creation, whereas I think about what the future holds and how we are going to grow into that environment.

There is a lot of talk about management – is it learned or innate? Every school that teaches MBA courses makes assumptions it can be learned and, indeed, a lot can be learned. In order to succeed you have to have a deep need to be great at management. Management is not just about leadership. Organisation of staff into logical units is clearly a vital general management attribute. Planning and controlling according to that plan are other necessary components. Learning all the time, about technology, customer choice, what the leading competitors are doing, is an essential part of the CEO's job.

When I did my Masters in industrial engineering in UCD (jointly with an MBA) I learned a phenomenal amount – that mixture of strategy and psychology which is essential for good management. I find psychology infinitely fascinating. When dealing with people you have to understand how they work and think, have an insight into the wellsprings of human motivation and how the levers can be operated in order to get people pulling in the same direction.

Recruitment is one of the most important functions in any company. Different companies use different methodologies. We use a combination of interviews, references and psychological tests. If you want really good and decent people, you have to treat them decently. You retain them because their set of values overlaps with your set of values – and when you're recruiting you try to select people with your set of values.

A chemical engineering classmate, Gerry Fahey, came to me in 2001 with a proposal that I found immediately interesting. Gerry had abandoned engineering and management for the study of psychology in his 50s. He was an exceptionally brilliant guy and we had remained good friends since we left college.

The proposal he made was for a test that merged the five genetic components of personality with three measures of intelligence. He had studied psychology at the University of Illinois at Champagne. The five genetically inherited psychological traits are summarised in the acronym OCEAN.

O stands for Openness
C stands for Conscientiousness
E stands for Extraversion
A stands for Agreeableness and
N stands for Negative affect or Neuroticism

Each of these has a series of sub-traits.

Psychological testing is based on the fact that individuals know themselves better than anyone else. The test allows them to describe themselves under these five categories. It is not time bound. Gerry specifies a range within which a candidate's score should fall. For instance, someone whose N score exceeded 83 would not be recommended for employment. The A score would ideally fall in the range 115 to 136.

The psychology parts of the timed test are put together with the AH4 and Raven measures of intelligence. A composite score, expressed as a percentile, is a great guide to how someone will perform on the job. It is, of course, capable of being manipulated, and a BIDR score is included. This compares answers to various questions and tells us if someone is faking. Any score higher than 10 in the BIDR indicates that a candidate is giving a set of answers that he thinks is what the assessor wants to see rather than accurate answers about his real opinion of himself.

Gerry has explained how the best predictor of success in any job is the candidate's intelligence. I could take hundreds of examples of how the test worked as a predictor of work behaviour, but one will suffice to show its value.

When Mainstream moved into a new country we bought out an existing small development company. We persuaded the people who had come from that company to work with us to do the OCEAN test. One of them got a high score on hostility (a subset of N) and straightforwardness (a subset of A). This person's natural trait was to be hostile to most people. It would have been inherited from his forebears, who confronted the wild animals and won and got to re-produce, thus preserving the hostile trait for future generations. In business high hostility combined with high straightforwardness is a disastrous combination. Not only did that person dislike nearly everyone with whom he came in contact, but he let them know it. Floods of abusive emails and confrontations ensued, until a parting of the ways was the only option open to the company.

Personality traits are like default settings in humans. Intelligent people can compensate for inappropriate traits when they are not under pressure. People can exhibit good behaviours when doing or-dinary tasks. Although these traits can be hidden in everyday be-haviour, it is when the person comes under pressure that they can be seen most clearly. That is what lies behind the Peter Principle. This says that people are promoted to the level at which they become incompetent. This can be related to intelligence, but it also is related to inherent personality traits. I saw the effect that stress can have on people. We had a staff member who had low conscientiousness. It is quite odd to find someone with this trait so I was intrigued to see how he would behave. When working in a team-based unit with lots of support this person appeared to be the most conscientious of them all, late hours, good results etc. He applied for a job abroad. In the new job he was more isolated, lacking some of the supports he had had formerly. He had to write a report. It was rubbish. The research done was harmless, based on one interview. The OCEAN test had been a good predictor of this behaviour. It is not just the overall result of the OCEAN test that matters; each sub-trait is important when it comes to predicting human behaviour.

The number of tests done by prospective employees has now run into the thousands, and they were a bad predictor of behaviour in only a very few cases.

Before Gerry, a big influence on me in these matters was the aforementioned Sean Brophy, who helped me at BNM with change management. It was a challenging process as, apart from Brendan Halligan, most of the senior management did not welcome having an outsider foisted on them. Brophy had worked in human resources with AIB and he instilled in me the importance of a sense of purpose. If you make staff feel they are involved in something more fundamental than just earning a wage, it gives them a sense of purpose, which comes mainly from within. Linking people's work to contributing to the environment, enriching the community and making their lives more meaningful in some broad societal sense helps create a more purpose-filled working life.

Sean used different psychological constructs to describe human nature. These are explained in *Strategy of the Dolphin*, by Dudley Lynch and Paul L. Kordis.[32] These constructs reinforced my belief that creativity, rather than brute application of force, was the way to win at business.

You can measure sense of purpose: Sean did this by conducting a test that concluded whether a person was 'on purpose' or not.

He performed another task to determine whether someone lived in the past, present or future. In this, or I suspect in any business, it helps if you look to the future, but I do that by nature anyway.

---

32 Dudley Lynch and Paul L. Kordis, *Strategy of the Dolphin: Scoring a Win in a Chaotic World*, New York, NY: Ballantine Books, 1998.

I live in the future and on occasion that presents communication difficulties with those who live either in the present or past. It can manifest itself, according to others, in jumping to conclusions. My father often accused me of this. I tend to jump from A to M, whereas many people need to proceed from A to B to C and so on.

This adventure in psychology enabled me to understand the way people think. It is easier to manage people if one understands what makes them tick.

Change is always hard, even for choice-seekers like me, because you get used psychologically to operating in a certain way. However, when you find that way is not very productive, or that it used to be but isn't any more, you have to change, to adjust.

We had in Airtricity, and we have in Mainstream and SuperNode (see page 163), an important role to play in leading this once-off, global transformation to sustainability. It's a tough ask. We need the best young brains and muscle to accomplish the task. We place a great emphasis on getting the best and the most determined people to work with us.

CHAPTER 14

Policies and People

When a new venture in the electricity sector is being planned, politicians' interest is profoundly captured. Security of energy supply is one thing that they take very seriously. Whenever there is a power outage that leads to citizens' inability to heat, cook and light their premises, politicians are called to arms by the affected citizenry.

I recall an incident in 1974 when Conor Cruise O'Brien, Minister for Foreign Affairs, somehow got through to the Pigeon House where I was working, and I was put on the phone to him. Apparently there was a power outage in his constituency and he wanted to know when the power would be restored. I was operating on the generation side and was unable to help him with any detailed information about his locality. He had simply called the wrong part of the ESB. I was able to reassure him that my power station was producing at maximum output, and gave him a number to call to get the facts about his local outage.

When the wind industry started up in Ireland, it was not welcomed by the monopoly supplier at the time, the ESB. Very few people were aware of the looming global warming crisis, and wind was seen as a kind of strange peripheral activity. Ireland was in no way unique in this regard. The incumbent companies involved in electricity generation supply could see their monopolies coming under threat from the new entrants into the market.

In Germany, where one would have expected a generally pro-environment response, the largest electricity company, E.ON, objected to the federal government's endeavours to introduce wind energy. The government had introduced a renewable energy fixed price feed-in tariff (REFIT) for wind installations. E.ON took their objections to court, arguing that favouring one generation over another was 'state aid', which was not allowed under EU rules. The case finished up in the European Court of Justice, where the judges found in favour of the German government.

At about the same time the Irish Transmission System Operator persuaded the regulator to put a moratorium on new wind connections to the system.

A company such as Airtricity therefore had to have a strong lobbying capability. Not only had policy documents to be prepared and submitted to the Departments of Energy and the Environment, but high-level meetings were a part of the job description of the senior management, in particular the CEO. Whenever we entered a new country the policy framework for deploying the new technology had to be agreed with civil servants and ministers.

We started in South Africa with a meeting with Cyril Ramaphosa, the future president. In 2000, he was appointed to the Independent International Commission on Decommissioning as an arms inspector, responsible for supervising decommissioning of Provisional IRA weapons.

When I met Cyril he was marginally involved in politics. He had a great sense of humour, and recounted many stories about arriving at Dublin Airport and being whisked away to various IRA arms dumps. The Irish Special Branch would have loved to know where the dumps were located, and cars were exchanged in tunnels to ensure that they weren't being followed. We were not able to do a business deal with Cyril.

When we introduced the concept of building wind farms in South Africa we met with ministers and civil servants. At the first meeting with the civil servants they explained that South Africa was a coal country and there was not much wind there. I was disappointed with this reception, and in a subsequent television interview I said I thought that many sections of the South African government were interested in renewable energy developments, but the Department of Energy didn't seem to be. This led to me being denounced by the Energy Minister, Dipuo Peters. A few years later I became reconciled with Dipuo at a friendly meeting. She was very much in favour of renewable energy at that stage.

At the second meeting with the Civil Service the same official told me that there was too much wind in South Africa!

Chile was the second country we entered and we went through a similar set of government interactions there. In 2016 I met with President Michelle Bachelet of Chile. I explained to her that I had recently visited Chassagne-Montrachet in Burgundy where her great-great-grandfather, Louis-Joseph Bachelet Lapierre, had come from. A French wine merchant, he had emigrated to Chile with his Parisian wife, Françoise Jeanne Beault.

President Bachelet had seen the price of electricity fall from a starting price of around $130 per megawatt hour to around $50 as a result of the building of wind and solar plant there. The meeting was long and cordial, and I found her to be a charming and welcoming person.

I had conceived of the Supergrid idea in 2001, initially to compensate for the variability of wind. As a result of readings from the University of Kassel in Germany, which pointed out that the wind was always blowing somewhere, I devised the Supergrid concept (see page 100 for an idealised representation of the Supergrid).

The logic of such a grid was apparent to most people. UK Prime Minister Tony Blair was a particular fan of the idea. He could see that, with the UK's enormous exposure to the shallow North Sea, it would be possible for the UK not only to supply all its own needs but to meet a good portion of Europe's electricity needs as well. I met him in the House of Commons in 2007.

I had been prepared for the meeting by Jeremy Haywood, who had been the PM's private secretary for many years. Jeremy, who died in 2018 at the age of 56, was working with Morgan Stanley, on sabbatical leave from the Civil Service. Airtricity had interactions with many of the major financial institutions, and it was through one of these meetings that I met Jeremy. He was a truly friendly and engaging person. I told him that Alasdair McDonnell MP had arranged for me to see the PM. His first question was, 'What are you going to say to the PM?' I said I would begin with global warming and go on to describe the Supergrid. He said, 'No, he knows all about global warming. What will you say about nuclear?' I said I was not there to talk at all about nuclear, just the Supergrid and renewable energy. To which he replied, 'Good, you want to talk about the 75% that is non-nuclear.'

Alasdair McDonnell studied in UCD along with me and we had become acquainted when I ran for president in 1968. He was leader of the SDLP in northern Ireland, and was very helpful in organising meetings with MPs. Alasdair was and is an absolute gentleman.

The meeting with Tony Blair lasted 15 minutes. He was all smiles at the start, but immediately dived in with the question, 'What do you want?' He asked about 15 questions and struck me as understanding everything I said. He was supportive of the Supergrid, and promised to raise the issue with Angela Merkel when next they met. After 14 minutes and 45 seconds precisely, one of his staff came over and pointed to his watch, and the meeting ended. When asked later in the House of Commons by Alan Whitehead, MP for Southampton West, if he had raised the issue with Merkel, the PM confirmed that he had.

Alex Salmond, the former leader of the Scottish Nationalists, was someone with whom I had a strong personal relationship. At the time of writing there are many allegations of sexual abuse being levelled against him, but I was completely unaware of any of these when we were in contact. Alex is a wholehearted believer in the Supergrid. He chaired a meeting of the Friends of the Supergrid in Edinburgh while he was First Minister. Without question, he is the most charismatic leader I have had the pleasure of working with. He is utterly dominant, charming, energetic and determined. For him offshore wind is the most important key to Scotland's future prosperity. He saw the Supergrid as the vehicle that would allow Scotland to export its electricity to continental Europe. It would render Scotland less dependent on the English market, which, from a Scottish nationalist's viewpoint, was to be welcomed. He has left a deep mark on the political history of the UK.

Alex's whole personality stands in sharp contrast to that of Al Gore. I was invited to a private conference in New York hosted by Gore. Along with some of his staff, he seemed to be the only audience. I presented a picture of the Supergrid at the conference. I saw none of the enthusiasm with Al that I had experienced with Alex or Blair. Perhaps this could be explained by the fact that he is an American and there are strong cultural differences between Europeans and Americans. Perhaps not. I found that vitality, that huge determination, to be a missing ingredient. He has written several books on the need to combat global warming, and for that he has to be applauded. I suspect that intellectually he is one of the more able advocates of the need to stop using fossil fuels, but in personal interactions and emotionally there is a slight lack. He is a Nobel Prize winner and deservedly so. However, I would have loved to see a little more passion.

In sharp contrast to Tony Blair, former UK PM David Cameron occupies a unique position in the history of the country. Whereas Blair was and is a committed European, Cameron always came across as ambivalent on this and almost every subject. During his first term as PM, he was seeking to build alliances in the EU with the Nordic countries. A meeting of the PMs of Finland, Denmark, Sweden, Latvia, Estonia and Iceland was arranged at Downing Street. A high-level delegation from the UK was organised to meet with business people and politicians from those countries.

For this particular conference I was approached to be part of the UK delegation. Both Airtricity and Mainstream were the leading developers of offshore wind, having developed the Greater Gabbard (650MW), Hornsea (3000MW) and Neart na Gaoithe (450MW) sites. This arrangement would have been put in place by Jeremy Haywood, together with Minister for Energy Charles Hendry, his good friend. Both wanted to see the Supergrid built and saw this meeting as a chance for me to present the concept to Cameron. There were addresses from the various PMs, after which there was a lunch hosted by George Osborne, Chancellor of the Exchequer, at No. 11. The presence of an Irishman on the UK delegation was an indication of the openness of the UK to foreigners. If you have something to offer they are delighted to see you. It came as a bigger surprise to me to be asked to speak at the lunch on the subject of offshore wind. There was no preparation for it and I had to wing it with enthusiasm.

In the afternoon the organisers had me present to the PM on the subject of the Supergrid. I emphasised the value that would be created by having the UK manufacture and sell large quantities of electricity to a green, power-hungry Europe. I recall that the CEO of Vattenfall, the large Swedish utility, also presented his views on on the unique problems of supplying electricity from a wind turbine on a small island where there was no back-up power, as would be the case on a mainland. One needs to make use of expensive batteries or inefficient diesel generators. After the presentation the PM suggested that I visit Oliver Letwin and discuss the Supergrid with him.

Letwin was a kind of minister without portfolio. He shot down the idea of the state having anything to do with setting up a policy regime that would allow electricity trading with Europe. 'Why don't you build the Supergrid yourself?' he asked. I explained that without a policy framework it would be impossible to do. The Germans or the Dutch could simply refuse to purchase the electricity, for any reason whatsoever. I explained that it would cost some £30 billion to build, and no company would spend this money without guaranteed access to foreign markets. It was a very short meeting and goes down in my life as one of the rudest I have attended. Clearly Cameron didn't like the idea of enhanced trading with Europe, even if it created opportunities for UK businesses and would have resulted in tens of thousands of new forward-looking jobs; but he didn't tell me this himself. It came as no surprise to me when he proposed and lost the Brexit referendum.

While the Neart na Gaoithe project was progressing at snail's pace through the Scottish labyrinth I had the opportunity to meet Nicola Sturgeon, Salmond's successor as Scottish First Minister. She has a legal background and this became very evident at my meeting with her. Clearly there would be a lot of employment from the construction and operation of Neart. She very much favoured the development but said she couldn't interfere with the planning process, which was independent of political influence. I could understand this, but I had to explain to her just how cumbersome, costly and under-developed the Scottish planning system was. She struck me as fundamentally straight and undogmatic. Her staff were also very supportive of the project and she was helpful in bringing the project to a successful conclusion.

I was once invited to Buckingham Palace to meet with the Queen and Prince Philip. All manner of Irishmen and women were assembled to meet them in their preparation for the visit of Irish President Michael D. Higgins. For a couple in their 90s they are amazingly fresh and lively. There were about 300 of us. The royals worked the room separately. I was chatting with a group of four others when Prince Philip joined us. He wanted to know what each of us did. I explained that we did renewable energy, and particularly wind in the UK. He immediately came back with the retort, 'But that doesn't work, electricity has to be made with nuclear.' I told him that was very expensive and would have loved to have had a debate with him about the whole subject. However, he was gone and we never had the debate. Despite this, I have to say I was immensely impressed that this elderly couple had the interest and the energy to engage with so many people in preparation for the president's visit.

Of all the PMs, presidents, princes and ministers I met, the most fascinating by far was the Asantehene, king of the Ashanti. The kingdom of the Ashanti is a large geographic area in the centre of Ghana. The principal town is Kumasi, a city of about a million people, and is where the Asantehene has his residence. I was introduced to the king by Lovelace Prempeh, whom I had met through a mutual contact in South Africa.

The kingdom of the Ashanti has been in existence since 1681, and has withstood intertribal strife and colonisation. Most unusually, the next king is chosen by the queen mother, so the succession is matrilineal. She makes a choice and her nomination is submitted to a council of lesser kings. I understand that her recommendation is always accepted. When the late queen mother died at 107 years of age I inquired how the next king would be chosen. It was explained to me that the king appointed a female member of the royal house with the title of Queen Mother. No son of the king can become king. Lovelace Prempeh's father was the Asantehene before the current king. The only way to keep the king in the same broad family was to avoid the transference of father to son. Coyly it was pointed out that the existing king could marry an outsider and she could have a son, but you could never be sure where he came from.

The Asantehene is traditionally enthroned on a golden stool known as the Sika Dwa Kofi, and the office is sometimes referred to by this name. When crowned, the king is said to be enstooled.

The Ashanti kingdom is one of the richest places on the planet in terms of natural resources. It has been mined for gold for centuries – Ghana was called the Gold Coast during colonial times. Gold mining is still carried out now but many of the gold mines have moved underground.

When the British invaded Ghana the Asantehene, Agyeman Prempeh, surrendered because he knew there would have been slaughter otherwise. Together with other nobles he was dispatched to the Seychelles for a number of years. In January 1902, Britain finally designated the Ashanti kingdom a protectorate. In the mid-1920s King Prempeh was allowed to return and was offered a palace by the British. He refused to accept this palace and built his own new one. It is a matter of conjecture what Africa would have turned out like had there been no colonisation and abstraction of slaves. If the Ashanti model of civilisation had grown throughout West Africa, we could have seen an alternative cultural construct, stable and progressive, to rival that of Europe or China.

The present king, Osei Tutu II, is a deeply impressive man. I met him on several occasions in connection with building renewable energy plants on Ashanti lands. He was educated in England, and before being nominated as the Asantehene in 1999, was an estate agent and a successful businessman. He has been visited by the Pope in Kumasi, even though he is not a Catholic. He has intervened successfully in tribal conflicts in northern Ghana. In 2019 he addressed the UN General Assembly. He has no tax-raising ability, but is very wealthy. In a sense all the land of the Ashanti is owned by him and the kingdom's lesser chiefs.

Energising the EU with Innovation

One of the most urgent necessities for the human species right now is the drive to decarbonise the atmosphere and end our dependence on fossil fuels. A historic accord was reached in Paris in 2015, under which almost 200 countries committed to reduce the consumption of fossil fuels, so as to contain the rise in atmospheric temperature to 2°C. Yet very little progress has been made since the signing of the agreement. In fact, global emissions of CO_2 have increased each year, plateauing in 2019 with an additional 33 to 37 billion tonnes of CO_2 being added to the global atmosphere. The reasons for this make for an interesting commentary on political systems and the workings of vested interests.

The EU has enough renewable resources within its geographical area to replace the use of fossil fuels. However, for most countries, these resources may not be within their national boundaries.

The optimum source of wind power is in the seas around Europe, particularly the northern seas and the Atlantic Ocean. For solar there is huge potential around the Mediterranean basin.

If European countries cooperated to harness these resources, they could meet all our energy needs in perpetuity. The absence of a plan to capture this renewable energy, which is clean and now cheaper than that generated by fossil fuels, is primarily down to a failure to innovate.

Decarbonisation in Europe requires the complete electrification of the energy system. We already know that transport and heating can be run efficiently and renewably using electricity. That 19th-century invention, the internal combustion engine, is an outdated, inefficient user of primary energy. The energy inherent in petrol or diesel, when burned in an internal combustion engine, turns only 16–21% of this potential chemical energy into motion. It can be replaced by batteries and electric motors, which work at efficiencies of around 90%. Most vehicle manufacturing companies now offer electric models, and it is anticipated that by 2050 all private and commercial goods vehicles will be electrified. This move will increase the demand for electricity in Europe by an estimated 1,385 TWhrs (terawatt hours) per year, which is roughly 40% of the current total electricity demand.

Switching to renewable energy for all heating is simple enough, in that no great shift in technology is needed. There is a whole variety of radiators, space heaters and heat pumps currently on sale. If all of Europe's heating were to be supplied by electricity there would be a need for an additional 3,158 TWhrs per year – around 90% of the current demand for electricity in Europe. Heat pumps are being deployed in Europe. They concentrate and pump heat from the surrounding environment into homes and offices. The energy (electricity) used to do the concentration and pumping supplies 300% more heat than the heat that goes into the heat pump.

If Europe were to decarbonise completely, demand for electricity would increase by an estimated 250%, going from the current 3,100 TWhrs to 7,800 TWhrs each year. These calculations are known to the EU authorities, yet there is no sign of any major initiatives being brought forward to prepare for this once-off transition, which is so badly needed to combat climate change. This failure to innovate is merely a continuation of former failures. Compared with the US and China, the EU comes in a distant third when it comes to promoting innovation.

The norm for the EU commission is to appoint large consortiums, with participation by competing companies, consultants, service suppliers and academics. Few companies are prepared to reveal their intellectual property in such a setting. Staff attend the consortium meetings in the hope that they can learn what competitors are doing, making sure they reveal none of their internally generated intellectual property. It is not surprising that very little 'innovation' emerges from these consortiums. They seem to be set up to encourage inter-country cooperation, as distinct from coming up with, developing or deploying new technologies. As usual, entities that have double bottom lines fall between two stools, accomplishing neither.

In 2018, 50 of Europe's biggest companies met and agreed among themselves that the EU was broken. They had all observed this collection of nations splinter into a number of segments since the economic crisis of 2008. Some of the criticism was echoed in the UK debate that preceded Brexit, particularly the attitude towards innovation.

The current EU is divided along north-south and east-west lines. The big companies saw how Germany had persisted in its century-old fight against inflation, from 2009 to 2014, five years after inflation had been replaced by deflation. The years 2010 to 2015 were really tough for Mainstream. Confidence in the Eurozone, dominated by Germany, evaporated. It was virtually impossible to raise money, which, for a capital-intensive company like Mainstream, could have been fatal. Austerity was the norm as Europe languished. There would be a high price for Europe to pay in the succeeding decade. Low economic growth, high unemployment, an exacerbation of the north-south divide and Brexit were consequences of this German-led conservatism. It wasn't until 2012, when Mario Draghi asserted the independence of the European Central Bank, and engaged in Quantitative Easing (QE), that the Eurozone began to grow. In contrast, the US introduced QE in 2009 and its economy has been growing each year since.

A huge mistake was made in Europe, however, when Angela Merkel, formerly a strong advocate of nuclear energy, did a complete about-face and, on 30 June 2011, she ordered the immediate shutdown of eight of the country's 17 reactors. The decision also outlined a timeline for taking the rest of the nuclear plants offline by 2022. There may be some more ill-advised decisions than this, but I don't know of them. They closed some nuclear plants and gave dates for the remainder to be closed. They almost bankrupted E.ON and RWE, and replaced the missing generation with brown coal generation. Emissions in Germany went up despite the building of more wind and solar.

One example of failure to innovate in the energy arena is that the EU had not foreseen the need for battery storage. As a result, a mere 3% of world manufacturing of lithium ion batteries happens in Europe. This is not nearly enough to supply the needs of the very large European car-manufacturing sector, which employs nine million people. With the world on its way to electrification of the motor fleet it is extraordinary that the EU and Germany should have allowed a situation to develop where a key ingredient would be sourced from foreign competitors. In 2018 Commissioner Maros Sefcovic was forced to announce a plan to spend some €2 billion on aiding the EU to increase lithium ion battery manufacture. An attempt is clearly being made to play catch-up with China and the US.

This inability to innovate has led to the situation where it will not be possible for Europe to meet its commitments under the Paris Accord. Whether it is carbon neutrality or complete decarbonisation, the EU has no plan to achieve either of these scenarios. Yet the solution is within its grasp if it were to devise ways both to avail of its renewable resources and to cope with the variability of wind and solar power. There is no strategy to suggest how Europe will capture the 900,000 offshore megawatts that have to be installed to meet the demand for the future enhanced electrification detailed above. There is also a need to install some 900,000MW of solar PV around the Mediterannean. There are no plans for the linking of these great resources.

The absence of a plan cannot be laid entirely at the door of the EU. Member states are continuing with installations of renewables strictly within their own boundaries. Local development of renewable energy plants was the right thing to do when their contribution to the local national electricity markets ranged up to 35%. Up to that level there was sufficient capacity on each country's electricity grids, which were built for fossil fuels, to accommodate renewables. If they're supplying more than 35%, the variability of renewables becomes a serious issue that requires a plan.

Wind and solar are energy sources that are variable and intermittent. They cannot be relied on. When there is an oversupply on the system, either the electricity that is being generated has to be shipped to another country, or the output from the wind turbines or solar plant has to be lowered. This 'constraining off' increases as the oversupply of renewable generation increases. When the output is constrained off the earnings from the sales of power is reduced. Constraining off is examined by the banks and equity providers when they come to look at funding for any new project. There is a relationship between the amount of renewable energy on the system and the number of constraints that will occur during the life of a wind farm. The more constraints the less income. The less income the more expensive the price for the reduced output. Because of this uncertainty about the output, banks refuse to fund projects at a certain stage.

There will be less constraining off if the electricity system is connected to neighbouring systems. With lots of interconnection penetration of wind can be higher. This is the case with Denmark. It sits between the bigger economies of Germany and Sweden/Norway.

There have been many occasions when electricity generated from wind in Denmark has exceeded 100% of demand there. Such luxury is not available to most countries, in particular Ireland. The degree of interconnection between Ireland and near markets is quite low.

As wind generators are paid for delivered electricity, developers progressively lose revenue because the grid turns off some of their machines. As a result, they cannot reach the return hurdle rates on their investments and they cease to invest. On the other hand, if the system guarantees to take all the renewable electricity produced, it has to take power it doesn't need and floods it on to adjacent markets. This is currently happening in Germany, from where electricity is spilled in an uncontrolled way into neighbouring jurisdictions. In addition, all the windy sites in Germany have been built on and the price of electricity has started to rise, because developers are being forced to build on less windy sites. The result of this local thinking is that wind energy on land in Germany, with a capacity factor of 25%, is priced almost identically to offshore wind energy in the UK, which has a capacity of 55%. It does not seem that Germany, or indeed any European country, has a plan to deal commercially with the variability of wind and solar.

Energy strategising has been plagued by propositions that are at best fanciful. Fusion reactors were supposed to be 20 years from commerciality in 1970, when I graduated from UCD. They are still 20 years from commerciality. In the middle 1980s it was reported that researchers had developed cold fusion in the laboratory. It proved impossible for other researchers to replicate the experiment. Then there is the thorium reactor, the hydrogen economy, carbon capture and storage, clean coal and even modern nuclear fission. All these suggestions have enough merit to warrant desk studies, but vast sums are currently being wasted on trying to commercialise them.

Take, for example, the hydrogen economy. The initial advocates of the hydrogen economy propose to make hydrogen by cracking water, which has the chemical formula H_2O. Renewable electricity is used to do this. The efficiency of conversion of the electricity into hydrogen is around 70%. If the hydrogen is then taken and put into an internal combustion engine to power cars, for instance, the efficiency of the conversion is further reduced by this old technology. If the world were to choose to go the route of the hydrogen economy, it would have to install six times as many wind- or solar-powered farms as would be needed if electricity only were used.

Another example is carbon capture and storage. This idea emerged when it was observed that pumping CO_2 down oil wells enhanced the recovery of oil. This tertiary recovery method can recover 30–60% of the oil from a field. There is a clear paymaster here in the additional saleable oil that is recovered. The fossil fuel industry floated the idea that the CO_2 emanating from a power station could be similarly captured and stored in holes in the ground. This is an impractical and extremely costly, not to say self-serving idea. The efficiency of the power station is reduced by 10% if the stack gases are interfered with. The reagent chemical that binds the CO_2 has to be bought. The resulting bound CO_2 then has to be transported to suitable holes in the ground. Costly logistics are involved in all parts of this process, and how can anyone be sure that the CO_2 will remain in the ground and not leach out over time?

This begs the question: Why would anyone build a coal-fired power station when the alternative wind and solar energy is so cheap? The CIA, which studies such things, reckons that the cost of a new coal-fired power station would have a levelised cost of energy over its lifetime of 9.2 $ cents. Mainstream is building wind in Chile for 4.1 $ cents, and in South Africa for 6 $ cents.

The reason for persistence with fossil fuels is largely vested interests. Additionally, natural human conservatism and ignorance of the facts play a role in bad decision-making. Perhaps the best example of vested interests is to be found in the behaviour of the

European Transmission System Operators (TSOs). With very few exceptions they refuse to reach out beyond their home jurisdiction to plan for a renewable future for the EU. Each TSO is a monopoly in its home area; in Ireland, it is EirGrid. Monopoly thinking is inherently anti-competitive and an innovative outlook is not the norm when making decisions.

Building grids is not recognised as a special assets class because it has been done by monopolies with little transparency of cost up to now. Monopolies fund their transmission grids from their own balance sheets, and usually receive a regulated rate of return. The buckets of money that have been poured into the generation sector of the electricity industry by private sector businesses don't as yet exist to fund the transmission expansion needed to support the transition to sustainability. Quite simply, there can be no transition without transmission.

The European TSOs come together in a cartel, the European Network of Transmission System Operators for Electricity (ENTSO-E). It is enormously influential with the EU Commission and Parliament. ENTSO-E's successful blocking of all progressive attempts to incorporate offshore renewables into a pan-European grid would make OPEC jealous. Their 'e-Highway 2050' solution is a collection of heavy transmission lines running on land in Europe. What international connections there are, are point to point. Just one offshore connection is shown and that is off the coast of France. The North Sea is not mentioned as a thriving offshore hub. The e-Highway report was a collaboration by 28 different groups, but no developers or private-sector grid builders contributed.

As I have said to my family, I believe I must play a leading role in getting Europe on the road to 100% renewables before I die. I believe the answer lies in my pioneering concept of the Supergrid, enabled by my newest commercial venture, the SuperNode company.

I want to build the Supergrid and the SuperNode before I depart this planet. I conceived of the Supergrid in 2001, having read some research from the University of Kassel in Germany, which stated the obvious: the wind is always blowing somewhere. If there was a grid long enough and broad enough, then the variability of wind would be partially compensated for. Initially I thought of this new Supergrid as only compensating for wind variability. As time moved on it was becoming clear that sea-based wind generation would be the norm. There is no grid in the sea so the Supergrid had a second and, perhaps, major reason to exist – the transportation of electricity from where it could be generated at scale to where the demand existed on land. It would resemble land-based grids in the sense that it would be meshed, providing multiple pathways for electricity to travel along, from generating station to the customer. This is necessary because failures or maintenance work could interrupt supply to some parts of the grid. To keep a reliable supply going to the customer an alternative route for the electricity to travel would be needed.

The big difference between onshore and offshore grids is the fact that the offshore grid is almost exclusively cable based. Overhead lines are not practical at sea. Direct current (DC) has to be used, whereas all land-based grids use alternating current (AC).

Thus, the Supergrid is a meshed offshore DC-based electricity transport system. The original SuperNode was the equivalent of a sub-station on land. It is a collector of electricity, and a router that directs the current towards where the demand exists at any point in time.

(The plan to develop the Supergrid will be the subject of a future book.)

CHAPTER 16

Africa's Future

Mainstream has been working in Africa for 12 years. During that time, I have become very concerned, not only with the energy situation, but with the entire future of the continent and all its people.

The European Political Strategy Centre set up by the EU is one of the most prestigious think tanks in the world. In 2017 it described the current state of Africa in these disturbing terms: 'Too much of the African continent is still plagued by a lack of decent basic infrastructure, slow growth, extreme poverty, pandemics, droughts, civil wars, terrorism and poor governance'.

The lack of infrastructure means that some 600 million people have no access to electricity. The main fuel for cooking is biomass, leading to an estimated 600,000 deaths per year. Because of poor governance economic growth is stagnating.

Extreme poverty means that while Africa has 12% of global population it only has 1.5% of global GDP. The countries of sub-Saharan Africa are the poorest in the world, yet the population is forecast to rise from 1.25 billion today to 2.5 billion by 2050. The UN forecasts it will increase to 4 billion by the end of the century, at which point Africa will account for 40% of the world's population.

Given that there is a failure to look after the current population, what is the prospect of being able to cater for a much larger population? At the purely human level we Europeans have a moral obligation to prevent a humanitarian disaster in Africa. We inhabit the same planet; we must help our fellow man.

It wasn't just altruism that attracted us to Africa. The continent is very rich in natural resources. We considered there was a commercial opportunity there for us, particularly in a country as developed and as stable as South Africa.

There was another reason to enter the African market. At the European level we have a strong obligation to protect our societies from the threat of mass immigration. If the stream of immigrants flowing into Europe were to increase dramatically, how would our democracies react? On current evidence, very badly.

Just look at what happened to the formerly popular Angela Merkel when her government accepted a million immigrants into Germany. Italy's perennial political instability has been worsened by the arrival of 500,000 immigrants. The political effects are not limited to Italy. Just think of Hungary and Austria, and even Scandinavia. Immigration is one of the root causes of the populism and deep divisions that now afflict the EU. For that reason alone, we need a major change in policy and we need it quickly.

A Marshall Plan for Africa

Having considered many options, I favour a Marshall Plan for Africa, which I first proposed in 2016 at the London meeting of the African Energy Forum. Since then, many others have proposed a similar sort of initiative, and I believe its time has come.

We Europeans could do what the Americans did for Europe after the Second World War. Led by wise leaders, the US had the foresight to recognise the importance of Europe in terms of its own self-interest. The goals of the Marshall Plan were to rebuild war-torn economies, remove trade barriers, modernise industry, improve prosperity and shore up democracy in the face of rampant communism. In effect, this would create functioning states in what was then a manmade desert.

I believe these goals are as relevant today in Africa as they were in Europe after the war. Under a new Marshall Plan, Europe would not only help in the development of the African continent but would also assist in creating a larger market for itself.

I am particularly encouraged by the fact that the EU and the African Union are working together on a new strategic relationship based on a mutuality of interest. However, as an engineer who has spent his professional life in the power industry I have a particular take on what needs to be done to help Africa reverse its fortunes, specifically, the electrification of Africa. I propose that it be done at speed by mobilising the resources of Europe to provide electricity for all Africans by 2050.

The rationale is simple – electrification is the key to industri-alisation, and hence to modernisation, and so to creating growth, wealth and jobs. Africa on its own can't build the power plants or the grids at the speed or on the scale required. We have to help, as President Macron proposed in his Sorbonne speech in 2017.

At present, sub-Saharan Africa has the lowest level of electrifica-tion of any region in the world. Leaving out the Republic of South Africa, it generates less electricity than Spain. While the annual per capita consumption of electricity in Ireland is just over 5,000kWh, in sub-Saharan Africa it ranges from only 700kWh in Zambia to as low as 61kWh in Uganda. That is ominously low, because elec-tricity consumption needs to exceed 2,000kWh per capita if an economy is to take off on self-sustaining growth.

Africa is nowhere near that point, as the table shows.

Table 1. *Energy Demand per Head in Different Countries*

Country	Population	Annual Electricity Consumption per capita (kWh)
Ireland	4,952,473	5,047
US	323,000,000	12,071
Germany	80,722,792	6,602
South Africa	54,700,704	3,904
Kenya	46,750,468	162
Ghana	26,908,262	341
Senegal	14,320,455	209
Ethiopia	102,374,644	65
Mozambique	25,930,150	462
Zambia	15,510,511	709
Zimbabwe	14,546,961	549
Cameroon	24,360,803	250
Tanzania	54,482,726	95
Ivory Coast	23,740,424	244
Namibia	2,436,469	1,518
Malawi	18,570,321	102
Mali	17,467,108	80

Table 2. *Electricity Consumption and GDP per Head by Country*

Country	Electricity Consumption per capita (kWh)	GDP per capita (US$)
Canada	14,350	46,200
USA	12,077	57,467
Australia	9,485	48,800
South Korea	9,165	37,000
France	6,986	42,400

Netherlands	6,920	50,800
Spain	5,230	36,500
China	4,310	15,535
South Africa	3,904	13,225
Turkey	2,087	21,000
Egypt	1,501	11,132
Vietnam	1,113	6,400
India	768	6,572
Ghana	341	4,294
Cote D'Ivoire	244	3,720
Yemen	211	2,500
Senegal	163	2,600
Kenya	162	3,156
Nigeria	115	5,900
Uganda	61	2,100

The Benefits of a Plan

What would be the benefits if Europe were to engage strategically with some chosen African countries? What if, instead of providing aid, or perhaps as well as giving it, Europe were to work with some African governments to enhance their capability to govern their own societies and to develop their economies?

We can look to Ireland as an exemplar. I have seen the beneficial effects of this country joining the EU. I have observed the great improvements in our standard of government, in the quality and quantity of our legislation, in the beneficial effects on the expertise of our civil servants through interaction with, and working in, Brussels. I am conscious, too, of the decrease in island-induced isolationism and of the opening up of Irish political, social and cultural attitudes as a consequence of being exposed to wider life experiences.

It was forecast back in the early 1970s that EEC membership would be a psychological liberation, and so it has been. The great growth experienced by Ireland since 1987 would not have happened if US industry didn't need an EU manufacturing base. Their first reason for choosing Ireland was membership of the EU.

The social and economic benefits have been beyond expectations, and would be worth replicating in Africa. That is why I favour a similar experience for Africa.

Electricity and Economic Growth

From the perspective of policy-makers the starting point is an unusual one, and requires some explanation.

There is a causal relationship between electricity consumption and economic growth, a point not generally recognised.

This is shown in Graph 2, but a better insight into the relationship comes from using the natural log of the data, seen in Graph 1. When presented in graphic format there is some scatter, but the trendline is obvious; there is a clear relationship between the per capita consumption of electricity and GDP per head.

The developed world is full of such examples.

In Ireland, the first major economic decision of the newly independent state was to pass the Electricity Supply Act of 1927, which established the ESB. Along with the construction of the Shannon hydroelectric scheme at Ardnacrusha, this act laid the foundations for the economic transformation of Ireland. A further necessary initiative made electricity available to every house and business and every town and village through the process of rural electrification. Today, Ireland has one of the highest rates of electrification in the world. It also has the fourth highest GDP per capita in Europe, and the fifth highest worldwide.

Singapore is a particularly good example. Half a century ago it was often compared to Kenya. Both were former colonies, and Kenya was held up as a good example of a relatively well-managed economy.

Graph 1. *Relationship between the per capita consumption of electricity and GDP per head.*

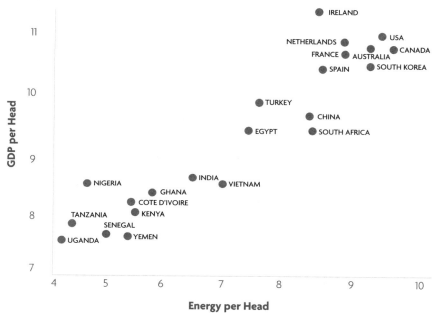

Graph 2. *Singapore vs Kenya GDP Growth per Capita*

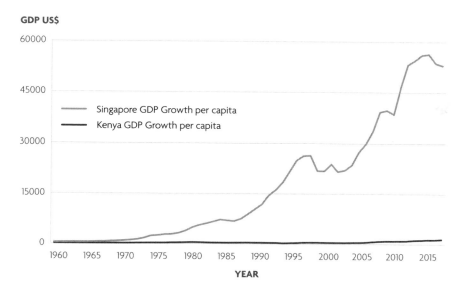

When Singapore gained independence from Malaysia in 1965, many of its three million population were unemployed, half were illiterate and per capita GDP was only US$516. Its first leader, Lee Kuan Yew, along with key ministers, visited Kenya in 1963 to study one of the most advanced post-colonial countries.

Singapore is now one of the world's richest states and Kenya one of the poorest. In Singapore, per capita GDP is $53,000. In Kenya it is $160. In Singapore, the per capita consumption of electricity is 8,845kWh, while in Kenya it is a mere 162kWh.

The facts speak for themselves – see Graph 2.

Of course electrification was not the sole reason for Singapore's economic transformation, but it was the necessary, indispensable precondition for economic take-off and sustained growth. In addition, there have been few political geniuses in history to rival Lee Kwan Yew.

Standard economic theory has no place for electricity when explaining the phenomenon of economic growth. This certainly surprised me. I was also taken aback that the UN Millennium Goals did not include electrification as a necessary precondition for promoting economic growth and social progress. These are just two examples of blindness on the part of economists and policy-makers. They are not alive to the central role of electricity in transforming society from the medieval to the modern.

Moving from mechanical to electrical power was the greatest paradigm shift in the history of civilisation and changed the very nature of society and the way we live. With the arrival of electricity economic growth became exponential, yet most economists neither recognise nor accept the causal link between electricity and economic growth.

In May 2008 a World Bank report said: 'Energy is necessary for economic production and therefore for economic growth but the mainstream theory of economic growth pays no attention to the role of energy; for example, the exogenous growth model where labour and capital are all that matters.'

This model, attributed to Solow, is still taught on economics courses and influences policy-makers when devising development plans for economic growth. It means they get it wrong. It's time to get things right because Africa has a huge problem with electrification – it's grossly underpowered.

The Role of the Entrepreneur

The underlying reason for the difference between Asian and African growth rates is usually overlooked by economists: the role of entrepreneurs and their dependence on electricity in order to function as business makers.

Entrepreneurs exist in every society, no less in Africa than anywhere else. Perhaps Africa has an abundance of entrepreneurs – any time I go there I am conscious of the vibrancy of society, of the small businesses being established, of the great cities from Accra to Addis whose streets are full of vendors.

However, if it has an abundance of entrepreneurs Africa has a shortage of electricity. As a result most entrepreneurs are self-employed rather than being employers. It can't be any other way because they don't have a 24/7 supply of electricity, so economic development is choked at birth.

Entrepreneurs are those precious people who take the business risk and who deliver the goods and services that consumers want. However, whether it's a shop, a garage, an office, a small manufacturing set-up, a transport company or a farming co-op, electricity is needed to get on with the business of doing business.

Due to the low levels of electrification, African entrepreneurs are disenfranchised. Until they are empowered like their counterparts elsewhere by having sufficient electricity there will be no growth in their economies. The small to medium enterprise is the foundation of all wealth creation and it is choked at birth in sub-Saharan Africa due to lack of electricity.

Africa's Problem

According to the World Bank, over 600 million people in sub-Saharan Africa have no access to electricity, and even for those with access to grid power, electricity is expensive and unreliable. The situation is dire. No electricity generation plant was built in sub-Saharan Africa in 2016 or 2017. In contrast, in 2017 China installed around 7500MW of wind and solar power. Given this state of stagnation it is no surprise that in sub-Saharan Africa manufacturing contributed less to GDP in 2016 than it did in 2005. This is illustrated in Graph 3.

Mainstream completed a wind farm in Senegal in 2020, one of the very few companies that has been successful in building wind plant in sub-Saharan Africa. A former employee of mine has won a contract for 40MW PV in Kenya, so I expect to see this built as well.

Solar PV is one of the great successes of the renewable energy revolution. The price has fallen dramatically since 2009 and, remarkably, is still falling. At an auction in Portugal in July 2020 the winning bid price was 1.4 $ cents. Not only can solar supply electricity in large quantities from huge arrays, such arrays can be thought of as power stations and deliver what is called utility grade power. One MW of a solar array occupies one hectare of ground. This is not the only contribution solar PV can make. Panels can be fitted to the roofs of buildings to supply some or all of the energy needs of the building. These panels can be retro-fitted to existing roofs, or, better still, the roof can be constructed at the building stage from photo-active tiles, which act like panels and generate electricity during daylight hours. In this way the very roof itself becomes a mini power generator. It is hard for me to understand why the political authorities do not mandate that all roofs must be constructed using photo-active tiles. However, while it may be possible to power individual houses using rooftop solar PV, manufacturing requires a 24/7 supply of reliable power, and so do services.

Graph 3. *Percentage Contribution of Manufacturing to GDP in sub-Saharan Africa*

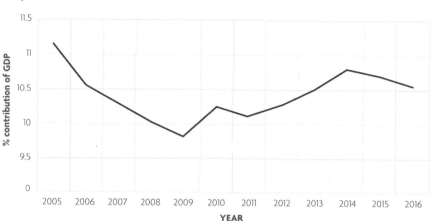

In order to deal with unplanned electricity outages African companies have to keep diesel generators on standby. These cost in the region of $400 per MWh, whereas large new wind and solar PV plants cost less than $100 per MWh. Thus, as a direct consequence of poor electrification, Africa's comparative advantage in low wages is offset by costly, inefficient and unreliable electricity.

So why has Africa not pursued electrification with relentless determination, as is currently the case in South East Asia? And in Ireland when she first achieved political freedom? Another historical precedent is the case of the US under President Franklin Delano Roosevelt. When he was trying to reflate the economy during the Great Depression, one of the first things he did was set up the Tennessee Valley Authority (TVA). During the First World War the federal government of Woodrow Wilson planned to build a dam on the Tennessee River, to supply energy to make munitions. However, the war came to an end and it did not get completed. It was only when FDR was trying to deal with the Great Depression that the dam got completed. FDR signed the Tennessee Valley Authority Act on 18 May 1933, establishing the TVA and giving it the authority to acquire lands along the Tennessee River and any of its tributaries for the construction of future dams, reservoirs, transmission lines or power plants. In 1936, when the Democrats had a majority in the House and Senate, FDR introduced the Rural Electrification Act. It brought electricity to every town and hamlet in the US.

With a generating capacity of approximately 35 gigawatts (GW), TVA now has the sixth highest generation capacity of any utility company. TVA's power mix as of 2020 is five coal-fired power plants, 29 hydroelectric dams, three nuclear plants (with seven operating reactors), nine simple-cycle natural gas combustion turbine plants, nine combined-cycle gas plants, one pumped storage hydroelectric plant, one wind energy site, and 15 small solar energy sites.

Perhaps the reason why African states haven't embraced electrification lies in the poor governance, which is a direct legacy of European colonialism in Africa. Most of today's national boundaries within Africa derive from the Berlin Conference of 1884–5, when the colonial powers divided the region between them. It is these artificial lines, rather than natural distinctions in background, culture or identity, that demarcate one African state from another. The colonial powers thus imposed artificial states on predominantly scattered tribal societies. Organic nation building has not happened in sub-Saharan Africa, at least in part due to colonial interference.

In attempting an explanation for weak state capacity throughout sub-Saharan Africa, therefore, one has to look at the diverse nature of African society. One piece of research found that there are as many as 3,000 different ethnic groups in Africa with about 2,000 different languages. Other research puts the figure higher. Thus, in terms of ethnicity, Africa is the most diverse of all the continents. There are 56 languages in Kenya and 80-odd in Ethiopia, to give just two examples.

The Greenberg Diversity Index is a measure of the chance that two randomly selected people would have a different mother tongue.

Out of the 25 most diverse countries 18, or 72%, are African. This includes 12 countries where Greenberg's Diversity Index exceeds 0.9, meaning that a pair of randomly selected people will have less than a 10% chance of having the same mother tongue. It's hard to build a nation when people can't talk to one another.

The primary language of government, political debate and public administration is often the language of the former colonial power: English, French or Portuguese.

This explains a key phenomenon about Africa. Instead of the gradual evolution of states as has occurred elsewhere, what we have today is the imposition of statehood on top of arbitrarily conjoined ethnic groupings, generally leading to conflicting loyalties and weak state capacity. Weak state capacity is arguably the main reason why Africa is not progressing and why it has not been electrified to any meaningful extent.

Weak state capacity means that the complex process of conceiving plans, putting them into action, and transposing them into sets of laws and regulations is beyond the ability of most of the countries in the continent. Although several African countries manage aspects of modern statehood well, most have neither the cultural framework nor the administrative skills to make the state work as it should. How else can we explain that no generation plant has been built these past two years? How else can we explain why electrification is so low in Africa? How else can we explain the many problems of sub-Saharan Africa?

We should address this situation in an innovative fashion because state capacity is key to Africa's future – and to ours.

Another issue that is particular to Africa and crucial to financing renewable energy, which is core to the electrification process, is land. It isn't possible to fund generating plant without land control, but in Africa land ownership is complex. Some land is owned communally, in some cases by nomads, in others by the government.

By and large, the European concept of private land ownership does not exist. This is as a result of the influence of climate on how society organises itself.

In rural Africa people didn't have to own land privately because it wasn't necessary for survival. The objective needs of feeding, housing and procreating were catered for by the extended family groups to which people belonged, without the bureaucratic and legal structures routinely found in the West. Yet clear legal title is fundamental to development and the Marshall Plan would have to work out legal mechanisms for reconciling communal and private ownership.

David Pilling, writing in the *Financial Times* about the 2017 Kenyan elections, noted that all the candidates were spending more on getting elected than they would officially earn during their entire period as parliamentarians. When Isabel Dos Santos was asked in an interview, 'How come you became the richest woman in Africa?' instead of saying that Daddy was the president of Angola, and insisted that a proportion of all mineral, oil and gas revenues went to his daughter, she answered 'talent'.

The rules of European society are designed to prevent corruption, not always successfully, but in Africa the cultural norm is for a chief or leader to enjoy a disproportionate share of the communal wealth and earnings, and this could explain why corruption exists in many African countries. It siphons wealth from the people and inhibits inward investment because corruption is an absolute no-no for western investors, although it has to be said that western companies often engage in corrupt practices and collude with native governments.

If anyone ever had doubts that corruption can destroy an economy the state of South Africa under President Zuma serves as a warning. Under Zuma's presidency, from 2009 to 2018, corruption became the norm. As they say in South Africa, 'the fish rots from the head down'. There was, under his leadership, not much difference between South Africa and the rest of Africa. It was characterised by endemic corruption, abuse of state assets leading to their failure, stagnant growth, collapse of the currency, civil strife resulting from huge wealth inequality, and high unemployment.

Since Cyril Ramaphosa took office it has emerged that corruption was rampant across all parts of the economy controlled by the ANC. The story of the wealthy Indian Gupta brothers, forging close ties with Zuma to plunder national resources, is the known tip of the corruption iceberg. Summed up by one US writer as 'a modern-day *coup d'état* waged with bribery instead of bullets',[33] this classic case of 'state capture', led to a three-year hiatus in the renewable energy programme. ESKOM, formerly one of the world's well-run electricity utilities company, became a special victim of Zuma-led, Gupta-executed skulduggery.

The sale of the Optimum coal mine is one example of this corruption. Glencore, the huge international mining company, received a letter from ESKOM telling them that their Optimum coal no longer reached the specified standards. Glencore put Optimum up for sale and it was bought by the Guptas. They paid for the sale by taking over the remelioration fund. This was not sufficient so they approached ESKOM for a loan. ESKOM lent them R560 million. ESKOM did not have enough money to do essential maintenance to their fleet generating plant, and the construction of two giant coal-fired stations at Medupi and Kusile was burning their capital at an alarming rate. Once the Guptas had bought the mine, its coal was suddenly acceptable, and met whatever standards there were. This is just one example of the Zuma-inspired kleptocracy.

Today, on the positive side, there are significant transfers of resources from Europe to Africa in the form of aid. OECD statistics indicate that US$54.2 billion in overseas development aid was transferred to Africa in 2016. Given the scale of the development

---

33   Karan Mahajan, *Vanity Fair*, March 2019.

problems, however, such aid merely scratches the surface and much of it could be characterised as sub-strategic. In order to effect the economic transformation that's needed, the approach must be strategic, with priority given to strengthening state capacity, eliminating corruption and electrifying the economy. That would be the agenda for the Marshall Plan.

That agenda would concentrate on the barriers to development and how to overcome them, but the process would have to be carefully thought out and built up gradually on the basis of experience – crossing the river by groping for stones, as Deng Xiaoping, the great Chinese liberator, said.

The process could begin by inviting certain qualified countries, carefully chosen, to enter into a bilateral relationship with the EU which would, of necessity, be treaty-based. They would then become exemplars for the others to follow. At its broadest, each treaty would seek to enhance the governance capability of the participating African country. Running the national treasury and dealing with issues like annual budgets, sovereign wealth funds, allowable debt levels, allocations of resources to productive uses as well as to health, education and welfare, and the design and management of infrastructural projects, would all form part of a methodology and technology transfer from the EU to the African participant.

The targets would be set out in multi-annual programmes and carefully monitored by the Commission, as it did with the Cohesion Funds Ireland received from the EU. Corruption would be measured annually. Money transfers would be contingent upon the achievement of target improvements in the transparency index, for example. Such measures would be objectively established.

The economic leg of the relationship would recognise that nothing positive will happen without electrification proceeding apace. The signs are encouraging, in that current wind and solar technology is capable of being rolled out quickly and the cost is between a third and half the price of coal. On the downside, the scale of the project is formidable.

Africa's average electricity consumption per capita was 770kWh as of 2015, which can be taken as the base year. So, if it is assumed that electrification means the provision of 2,000kWh for consumption per capita, the required level of wind and solar generation can be estimated as follows:

Demand was 920 TWh in 2015. With a projected population of 2.5 billion people by 2050, overall demand will rise to in excess of 5,000 TWh.

Assume that it will be met by wind and solar PV on a 50:50 basis. Africa would then require over 134,000 3MW wind turbines and just under 16,000 50MW solar farms (assuming 35% and 25% capacity factors respectively).

In 2017, the top 15 wind turbine manufacturers delivered approximately 20,000 wind turbines worldwide, with an average capacity of 2.4MW. This shows the scale of the work required for the electrification of the continent.

It should not be forgotten that India has similar ambitions, and the West is going to have to change all its fossil fuel plant during the same time scale, so competition for turbines and solar panels is going to be fierce.

It would be efficient and economical to install the new wind turbine manufacturing facilities required on the continent of Africa. So far only generation has been considered. Transmission and distribution must also be considered. National grids, at transmission and distribution levels, will have to be built.

That is one reason why we require the mobilisation of Europe's engineering and financial resources to help Africa provide electricity for all by 2050. This is an engineering project of significant proportions, but isn't that what we need to create employment? Africa's population is, after all, 2.5 times larger than that of the EU.

It is bigger than the US, Canada and the EU put together. The land area is immense. The distances to be covered are vast. So too are the numbers of people living in urban areas, who on average consume three times more electricity than those in rural regions. By 2050 Africa's population will be mainly living in cities and dependent on urban infrastructure that hasn't yet been built.

Like their counterparts in the West, African cities are growing in size and are experiencing social distress while relying on crumbling and ancient infrastructure and lacking a regular supply of electricity. These cities are already huge. Lagos has over 20 million people, Kinshasa has 13 million, and there are 10 other cities whose population is greater than the population of Ireland itself.

That explains why an essential preparation for the Marshall Plan would be to spell out the scale and pace of infrastructural development and to estimate the physical and human resources needed, especially in terms of materials, engineers, technicians, information technologists and, of course, finance.

Increasing security for European investors would be another key goal of the Marshall Plan. It should not be forgotten that some $70 trillion of largely western money is looking for good investment opportunities. They are put off investing in Africa, not least because of currency risk, in addition to corruption. That would have to be addressed and implies that the currencies of participating African countries would be underwritten by new global or EU financial arrangements.

We need to take immediate action to achieve success and prevent disaster. Let us in Europe recognise that we have a strong and growing interdependency with Africa and devise a new strategy, drawing on lessons of the Marshall Plan, to help Africa become master of its own destiny, with a little help from its European neighbours.

By 2100, five of the world's 10 largest countries are projected to be in Africa

Countries with largest population, in millions

Asia   Europe   Latin America and the Caribbean
Africa   Northern America

1950		2020		2100	
China	554	China	1,439	India	1,450
India	376	India	1,380	China	1,065
U.S.	159	U.S.	331	Nigeria	733
Russia	103	Indonesia	274	U.S.	434
Japan	83	Pakistan	221	Pakistan	403
Germany	70	Brazil	213	D.R. Congo	362
Indonesia	70	Nigeria	206	Indonesia	321
Brazil	54	Bangladesh	165	Ethiopia	294
UK	51	Russia	146	Tanzania	286
Italy	47	Mexico	129	Egypt	225

Note: Countries are based on current borders. In this data source, China does not include Hong Kong, Macau or Taiwan. Regions follow United Nations definitions and may differ from other Pew Research Center reports.
Source: United Nations Department of Economic and Social Affairs, Population Division, "World Population Prospects 2019."

PEW RESEARCH CENTER

This table shows a startling future, one that is difficult for me to accept. Nigeria is a byword for corruption, even by African standards. If it can't govern itself effectively with a population of 207 million, how will it cope with a population of 733 million? This is particularly concerning given that data (researched by Allwell Okpi) from early 2018 showed that oil contributed 87.7% to foreign exchange there. By 2100 the oil era will be well and truly over. Nigeria will have a bigger population than the EU. This projection alone demonstrates clearly why we Europeans need to act to help Africa.

Doing Business with China

I had always been fascinated by the collective culture of the Far East. When I was a CEO for the first time I looked around for models of good CEO behaviour. One that jumped out at me right away was the Japanese model employed by Konosuke Matsushita, an entrepreneur who built the great Panasonic corporation from his garage. He probably didn't invent the collaborative model on which all Japanese corporations are culturally based, but he was its initial most prominent and successful user. His philosophy went something like: 'You people in the West may be inventive and hardworking, but no matter what you do we in Japan will always win. We assemble all our people into a collective single being and this gives us considerable strength. Your internal competitive business way of behaviour, pitting staff against staff, managers against workers, just isn't able to compete with our collective model.' These are not his exact words, but they do express the way things were and are done in most Japanese companies. This thinking guided me, and gave rise to much of the way I choose to run businesses.

There was an incident involving my brother Dessie, which illustrates how Japanese culture works. Dessie is married to Yoko Ono (not John Lennon's wife) and they live in England. She used to teach and do research in a Japanese university before she married Dessie. They went back to her old university for several months' work. Upon arrival, they were told that the faculty was going skiing. Dessie said,

'That's great, have a good time.' The response was, 'No, Dessie-san, you don't understand, we are going skiing.' One in, all in.

I had encountered the Japanese Yamashita Shinihon shipping company when I was the fuel purchasing manager for the ESB. I had visited them in Tokyo in 1986 and been impressed with their levels of customer service.

In Airtricity we were always looking for new sources of capital, as we held on to all the plant we built. This tied up vast quantities of cash and meant we had to go back to the markets every 20 months or so. I went to Japan on several occasions during the Airtricity days. I met with most of the big trading houses – Mitsubishi, Sumitomo, Marubeni, Mitsui, to name but a few. None of them actually invested in Airtricity, but later on, in the Mainstream days, Marubeni made a significant investment of €50 million in the company.

During my college days I had come into contact with the student Maoists, who were very active in both my university, UCD, and in Trinity. They were very serious people, and they seemed to attract the brightest students. They really did believe in the words of the great Chairman Mao, and they were proud to carry around with them the Little Red Book containing his thoughts. They introduced a new vocabulary into the student political spectrum. It was here I heard about 'Comprador capitalism; running dogs of the lackey imperialists; cultural imperialism'. They loved the idea of the great Cultural Revolution, which was tearing China apart at the time.

During the 1960s the world became aware of what was happening in China. We had heard of the Great Leap Forward in the 1950s and the Cultural Revolution in the 1960s. China seemed to be run by the Gang of Four, one of whom was Mao's wife. Knowledge of how China worked and the philosophy that guided its culture and decision-making came much later.

The opening of China to the West came when President Nixon and Henry Kissinger visited the country in 1972. The week-long visit, from 21–28 February 1972, allowed a world viewing public to see China for the first time since the Communist Revolution led to the establishment of the People's Republic of China in 1949.

The real opening up of China had to wait for the death of Mao in 1976 and the ascension to power by Deng Xiaoping in 1978. Deng was as different from Mao as it is possible to get, while working within the same political framework. China, with its 1.2 billion people, began to interact strongly with the West. Foreign investment was encouraged, and the greatest transformation of any nation's wealth in world history was about to begin.

For the next 40 years the Chinese economy grew at an average rate of 10% per annum and 800 million people moved from dire poverty to average middle-class wealth. China also practised a 'one child policy'. In order to avoid a population explosion, the Chinese people adhered to the proposal by the government that families limit their size to one child.

Most western companies moved significant parts of their manufacturing businesses to China. At the beginning of Deng's transformation of the economy, and for 30 years, Chinese labour cost maybe one tenth to one quarter of equivalent work in the West. This had several major effects, including the political, economic and technological ones that followed from this easterly migration of manufacturing.

China is not like any other former colony. The ruling Communists knew exactly what they wanted from this willing invasion by western firms. They wanted, of course, employment for their people. However, they also wanted access to the knowledge – scientific, industrial, commercial and technological – underpinning this current manufacturing epoch and future epochs. As part of the deal that allowed the companies in, they agreed to share their intellectual property. Contrary to what some sections of western opinion now say, the multinationals did not have their intellectual property stolen. They shared it. They wanted to be able to generate higher profits, in the short term, so they agreed to the proposition. It was a relatively straightforward deal. Deng was aware of how heavily future industrial and business success depended on knowledge acquisition and its creation in the here and now.

I attended a colloquium at Harvard Business School in 2008, during which there was an open discussion on offshoring. As far as the academics and business people who attended were concerned, offshoring of manufacturing had been a great success. In fact, the major proposition under discussion was the offshoring of services. They were calmly discussing how 25–28 million jobs could be relocated to cheaper labour markets. I have to admit I was astounded by the tone and content of the proceedings. I pointed out that the current discussion could not take place in France, as a prime consideration for policy decisions in Europe would be the employment consequences of any major offshoring. The leader of the session was a little annoyed that Europeans didn't get the big picture. As far as I was concerned the only people who made any sense at the colloquium were the spokespersons from the AFLCIO, the US trade union movement. They asked the simple question: 'Who could afford to buy the services if so many people were unemployed?' I saw that what had been said for a long time was true: the business of the US is business.

I decided to explore the possibility of doing business in China, as I could see an explosion in demand for everything, including electricity. I first went there in 2004, and we opened an office in Beijing in 2005, during the Airtricity days. We constructed 27 wind speed-measuring masts in Inner Mongolia. The wind speed was terrific, around 9 metres per second. Inner Mongolia is an elevated area, quite similar to Texas in the US. It covers an enormous area of 1,200,000 square kilometres, with a low population of 25 million. It could have become the electricity-generating centre of

China using wind. If it were to be completely covered in wind turbines it could house some 12 million MW. Of course, this figure is theoretical only, as it would not be possible or in any way practical to cover any geographic area fully.

However, we did no business in China. The price for electricity there is too low for any foreign company to make an economic return. I learned of one New Zealand company that had formed a joint venture with a local company to develop renewable energy in China. It didn't succeed in making a profit and pulled out of the market. We closed the office in Beijing, but I remained in close contact with the turbine suppliers, Goldwind and Sinovel.

A fascination with Chinese culture had taken a firm hold of my imagination. I began to read the Analects of Confucius. This ancient Chinese text comprises a collection of sayings and ideas attributed to the Chinese philosopher Confucius and his contemporaries, traditionally believed to have been compiled and written by Confucius' followers. They form the basis of ancient and current Chinese culture and are radically different from the mainly Christian traditions of the West.

Confucius may have believed in ghosts or spirits but preferred to keep them at a distance. There is, in his thinking, no need to interpose a personal god into one's system of morals and behaviour. His political philosophy was rooted in his belief that a good ruler would govern his subjects through education and by his own example. 'If the people be led by laws, and uniformity among them be sought by punishments, they will try to escape punishment and have no sense of shame. If they are led by virtue, and uniformity sought among them through the practice of ritual propriety, they will possess a sense of shame and come to you of their own accord.'

There is the sense of mutual respect between the citizens and the ruler. They each have duties one towards the other. Much of this respect can be gleaned from another quote from the Analects.

'Tsze-Kung asked, "Is there one word with which to act in accordance throughout a lifetime?" The Master said, "Is not reciprocity such a word? What you do not want done to yourself, do not do to others."' The similarity of this to the advice that appears in Matthew's Gospel, 'Do unto others as you would have them do to you', is striking.

Chinese civilisation has been around and flourishing for probably 3,000 years. This, in itself, is unique in world history. Part of the reason for its continuity and longevity is the relative remoteness of the country. There are great natural barriers to any conquest of China. The vast wastes of Siberia, the Himalayas, the Hindu Kush, the Tien Shan range and the mighty Pacific allowed China to think out a political, social and cultural identity for itself. Once a culture was established there, it became embedded in the popular consciousness without wars to uproot the people and smash the cultural traditions.

China is the oldest meritocracy. There were examinations to select the best brains to join the bureaucracy and run the country. This arrangement fits with the philosophy outlined in the Analects. If one reflects on the nature of meritocracy, it throws up a conundrum. What if the brightest in society are from an unrepresentative elite? Will they not just rule in the interests of the top few? It seems to me that meritocracy, without a firm set of societal values, could be a recipe for repression, little better than theocracy, regency or autocracy.

That is the difference between the Chinese variant of meritocracy and others. There is a firm reciprocity between the governed and the rulers. This pact between the people and their government stands in sharp contrast to what is observed in the modern US, for instance. A promise to 'drain the swamp' in Washington was one of the effective slogans used to get Donald Trump elected to the presidency.

The Analects has this to say about societal order without the use of repression:

> Lead the people with administrative injunctions and put them in their place with penal law, and they will avoid punishments but will be without a sense of shame. Lead them with excellence and put them in their place through roles and ritual practices, and in addition to developing a sense of shame, they will order themselves harmoniously.

Chinese culture is so strong that it has survived indifferent imperial rule, Japanese and English invasions, the nationalist struggles of the early 20th century and the ascension to power of the Communists in 1949. Even throughout the Great Leap Forward, when millions died from starvation, and again during the Cultural Revolution, where ideology flourished over people's livelihoods, loyalty to Mao Zedong remained firm. It is hard to imagine any other country where the transition to a new way (Deng) of growing a country was so radically different from the one that had gone before. Yet Deng never openly criticised Mao, despite the fact that he had been banished to the countryside and worked as a fitter for four years and his son became a paraplegic after being attacked and thrown out a four-storey window by Red Guards. Nor has any subsequent leader criticised Mao.

I became interested in China, initially for commercial reasons. However, after becoming familiar with the culture, and full of respect for what was being accomplished in terms of economic growth, I made it a point of trying to explain it to myself. I concluded that China is going to be the major force in the world for the next century. Milestones along that path have already been achieved. The Chinese economy is nominally the second biggest in the world, but if economic size is judged in terms of what the people of a country can buy, in purchasing power parity terms, China bypassed the US in 2017. China has demonstrated a unique way for great powers to acquire foreign natural resources – paying for them. This stands in sharp contrast to all other imperial powers who, during their colonial phases, invaded countries and robbed their natural resources. The Belt and Road initiative, Xi Jinping's great $7 trillion achievement, will set up diverse trading routes with Africa, the rest of Asia and Europe.

When Deng took the reins of power he began to emphasise the goals of 'four modernisations': economy, agriculture, scientific and technological development and national defence. In 1982 he established a new Commission for Science, Technology and Industry for National Defence to plan for using technology that was being developed in the civilian sector.

One of the leading symbols of the success of Deng's scientific and technological initiatives is evidenced by the Huawei company. Their offering of 5G connectivity is leading the world. Nowhere can the fading power of the US be better observed than in the case of Trump trying to bully the world into not purchasing Huawei, falling out even with his greatest ally, the UK. Huawei has spent billions of renminbi and tens of thousands of man hours developing the underlying technology. As Newt Gingrich pointed out in his recent book, no US company has invested in a long-term future technology such as 5G.

For all of us in business, and for everyone not in business, China is a vital cog in all our economic futures. There are 1.4 billion people living in China. This is more than the US (330 million), the EU + UK (520 million), Canada (36 million), Japan (125 million), Australia (23 million), Mexico (129 million), Russia (141 million), Chile (18 million) and South Africa (59 million) added together. It is the fastest-growing economy, even if it has slipped from the dizzy heights of 10% growth per annum to 6–7%. It is not only part of a global manufacturing supply chain, it represents the biggest market on earth for goods and services from everywhere else. Trade wars with China are a policy mistake. There are much more effective ways to ensure a high trade reciprocity with China than a confrontational trade war. This trade war, launched by Trump, begins to resemble a real war insofar as the truth is the early loser.

At one point, Mainstream had to carefully navigate a situation with the second wind turbine manufacturing company we sought to deal with, Sinovel. One of their staff, a Croatian, stole intellectual property from AMSC (American Superconductors), and was arrested in Austria. I received a phone call from a 'trade representative' at the US Embassy in Dublin. He told me what I already knew, that Sinovel had been bad boys and that we should do no business with them. I told him that I was familiar with the case and would do what I had decided to do anyway, which was walk away from the relationship. I reckoned it would damage Mainstream if we bought turbines from a company that had been caught stealing. On my next trip to Beijing, I told our representative there, Wang Jun, to inform Sinovel that we couldn't honour our arrangement. The conversation happened in Chinese, and it got pretty steamy, although I couldn't hear what exactly was being said. We never did business with Sinovel.

We did, however, do good business with Goldwind, whose chairman is Wu Gang. I like this company. Using their equipment we built a 110MW wind farm in Illinois. Although it received little comment at the time or subsequently, this was a considerable achievement. There was no negative comment in any section of the US media, political or wind communities. The turbines are well made and have met output expectations. Goldwind acquired the intellectual property from German company Vensys in 2008 for a reported €45 million. It was advanced technology at the time, using permanent magnets. We also built a 35MW wind farm in Chile using Goldwind technology. This was our first wind farm built in an active earth-quake zone. It was supported by the Chinese Development Bank.

China, and its political governance system, is with us to stay, and it will stay because it works. The average family in China sees itself as embedded in the traditions and behaviours of countless former generations. It is an amazing fact that our Wang Jun's wife in China could trace her lineage back to Confucius 113 generations ago. No person in any other country could make such a claim. There is no personal god for the great majority of Chinese, but there is family. In a sense, what God gives to God-believing persons is life after death. The Chinese achieve life after death via their families. They don't worship their forebears, but they remember them with great honour and reverence.

For a country like Ireland, the rise of China creates a unique issue. All of Ireland's new-found wealth is founded on foreign direct investment (FDI) by a large number of US multinationals who couldn't sell their goods to any EU country if they didn't manufacture within one of the member states. Having studied each country they basically all decided to locate in Ireland. In addition to being a member of the EU, Ireland has a lower tax rate than any other European country. There is a stable political regime, English is spoken, there is a big pool of well-educated graduates, and the icing on the cake is that many of the managers' and owners' forebears hailed from Ireland. It is astounding that Ireland, comprising just 1% of the EU population, receives 90% of US FDI.

This mass investment began during the minority government of Charles Haughey in the late 1980s. What is less commented upon is the revival of this mass investment around 2014, when the new wave of US social media and IT companies began to locate in Ireland. This sparked a new period of unprecedented growth for the Irish economy, which lasted until the Coronavirus pandemic. A florid and probably stupid expression of this rate of growth happened in 2016 when the statisticians speculated that the GDP here had increased by 27%, giving rise to the term leprechaun economics, coined by Paul Krugman. This was the 26.3% rise in Irish 2015 GDP, later revised to 34.4%, in a 12 July 2016 publication by the Irish Central Statistics Office, restating 2015 Irish national accounts.

The mid-20% growth is not true. It arises from changes to the balance sheets of the multinationals, in which intellectual property was included. What is true is that Ireland has experienced 5–6% growth since 2014, far and away the highest growth rate in the EU.

Ireland occupies a unique position insofar as 32% of its wealth derives from manufacturing. This is unique among highly developed countries. The nearest country in Europe in terms of manufacturing contribution is the Czech Republic, with 23%. German manufacturing accounts for 20% of its wealth. In the UK the contribution of manufacturing is 9%. It demonstrates the conundrum for Irish politicians as the US seeks to create an anti-Chinese global momentum.

So far Ireland has ridden both horses with considerable success. During the early years of Mr Deng's opening and industrialisation of the Chinese economy, high-level officials were dispatched to various parts of the globe to study what led to their success. Jiang Zemin, future Secretary of the Communist Party, was one of the team sent abroad. One of the places he visited was Ireland. He discovered Shannon, or rather what the government had created at Shannon, Shannon Free Airport Development Company (SFADCO). SFADCO, which occupied the Shannon Free Airport Development Zone, set up by guiding founder Brendan O'Regan in 1959. The Chinese team saw an area, well separate from a Dublin bureaucracy, with its own entrepreneurial culture, special taxation arrangements, and the closest point in Ireland to the US with its free enterprise culture (on the old airline route). It also had access to nearby ports. It was eventually to become a thriving industrial area, with a new town, and soon its own university. Among the fine companies it spawned was Tony Ryan's GPA.

What the Chinese saw excited their imagination. They re-created Shenzhen in Guandong Province, just opposite Hong Kong, along the same principles that underlined the Shannon Free Area Development Zone. Shenzhen, up until the time it was declared to be a special development zone, was a relatively small border town, with a population of 30,000 inhabitants, mainly notable as a jumping-off point for Chinese wanting to get into Hong Kong. Now it is the Silicon Valley of China, with an estimated population of 25 million. All taxis there are battery-powered electric vehicles.

The links with Ireland did not stop with the visit of Jiang Zemin. Every Chinese leader since then has visited. In fact, the first European country that Xi Jinping visited was Ireland.

There is a newly built Confucius Institute on the UCD Campus. The professor of Chinese studies is Liming Wang. UCD itself has a joint venture operation in Beijing called Beijing-Dublin International College (BDIC), located at the Beijing University of Technology (BJUT) campus in south-eastern Beijing.

Ireland depends heavily on US multinationals for its continued wealth, and on a continuing strong relationship with the US administration, of whatever hue. However, we have to recognise that we are entering the Chinese century, when the dominant world force will be China. In a time of increasing tension Ireland must tread cautiously.

Since 2009, China has contributed to more than 30% of global economic growth, according to the statistics of the World Bank and other organisations. The creation of new knowledge had been understood by Deng Xiaoping as critical to the future wealth of China. It has accelerated its acquisition of new knowledge in the past 20 years. Before this time foreign multinational companies traded their current intellectual property for cheap labour and access to the Chinese market. They were delighted to do it, because they created super-profits, which, in theory, would have allowed them to invest more money in advanced R+D and so be ready for the next wave of commercial technology. Anecdotally they didn't do this. The EU, through its big successful companies, had a lead in new technology in the electricity space. Both ABB and Siemens had developed the DC circuit-breaker, but because of protectionism and lack of innovation it was never deployed in Europe. The Chinese have built on the initial intellectual property obtained from these companies and have deployed the DC circuit-breaker. There has been an explosion in new wind turbine (WTG) manufacturing companies emanating from China. This is in sharp contrast to what has happened in Europe, where there has been a contraction in the number of WTG companies. We are now down to four WTG companies, from 15 a decade ago.

Patents are one way of measuring the creation of new commercial intellectual property. In 2008, the Chinese authorities received 204,268 patent filings, compared with 428,881 in the US. However, in 2017, China's State Intellectual Property Office received 1.3 million applications – more than double the number received in the US, according to statistics from the World Intellectual Property Organisation, the global forum for policy in the field. According to David McCormick, chief executive of Bridgewater Associates, and former under-secretary of the Treasury in the Bush Administration, the US federal share of R&D spending hit a 60-year low in 2018.

Many large US companies have been buying back their shares, and increasing the share price. Much of the money that has been earned in low labour-cost areas has been used to buy back shares. In this way there has been a concentration of wealth, created as a result of having access to cheap labour, in those groups who owned shares. What is interesting with respect to share buybacks is the ease with which the share price can be increased. Instead of carrying out research and spending time commercialising it, a much quicker fix of the share price is to buy back the shares.

At the same time in the US many of the skills that created and sustained the Great Society have been lost. The baby boomer skill sets have not been replicated by the succeeding generation as the economy lurches towards a services-oriented one. This happened partially as a result of the offshoring of their industry. Crucially, since Ronald Reagan was president, funding for innovation and public education has also decreased.

We in Ireland should aim to be part of the Belt and Road initiative, which, although it has involved some not-so-green and also controversial elements, seems to be refocusing on technology and renewable energy at the time of writing. This should happen whatever the attitude of the EU towards China. It can be argued that as part of the Belt and Road initiative those countries that are connected to China can sell their produce there. Thus, US companies manufacturing here would have access to the biggest market on the planet. In that way we can use our neutrality, not in a negative isolationist manner, but as an honest broker between two contending behemoths.

CHAPTER 18

A Vision for a Decarbonised Energy Future

Changing to renewable energy represents a dramatic shift in human thinking. Albert Einstein once remarked that intelligence isn't enough; imagination is what is needed to make the critical breakthroughs. His image of riding on a wavelength of light helped him understand the concept of relativity, which turned Newtonian physics on its head.

Thankfully, this kind of breakthrough is not necessary to stop using fossil fuels. However:

1. We need to be able to put figures on the damage to human health and the overall costs of adding greenhouse gases to our atmosphere.

2. We need to understand the costs involved in making the transition, which depend on how quickly the costs of generating renewable energy and other technologies such as electricity storage are falling.

3. Not all countries are at a similar level of development, so any policy that is introduced has to take this into account. Bigger contributions have to be made by the more developed economies. A sense of equity has to prevail and be agreed among the nations.

4. There need to be uniform methods of accounting for each nation's contribution to mitigation, so that the individual nations' contributions can be measured and compared, and adjusted if necessary.

5. Voluntarism has failed as a mechanism to control the emissions of dangerous greenhouse gases. Nations are able to extract themselves from the Paris Accord without penalty, leaving others to carry the burden.

1. Quantifying the damage

Various estimates have been prepared by different groups over the past few years. The study quoted earlier, carried out by Greenpeace Southeast Asia and Center for Research on Energy and Clean Air, calculated that pollution from burning fossil fuels is generating economic losses of $8 billion a day.

That's about 3.3% of global GDP, or $2.9 trillion per year. China, the US and India bear the highest economic cost of soaring pollution, at an estimated $900 billion, $600 billion and $150 billion a year, respectively. The report says that 'Air pollution continues to harm billions of people on a daily basis, despite efforts by some countries and companies to push for greater use of renewable energy and cleaner fuels. Burning coal, oil and gas causes health issues, potentially leading to 4.5 million premature deaths around the world each year, with 40,000 children dying before their fifth birthday due to the exposure to fine-dust particles smaller than 2.5 micrometers, known as PM 2.5.'

Morgan Stanley reckons that 16 climate and weather disasters cost the US $309 billion in 2017 alone.

It is hard to associate a cost with the reduction in biodiversity that global warming entails, but there is a real cost, and ways have to be found to measure it and put a figure on it.

'Mi casa es su casa' is a Spanish phrase conveying the welcome offered to a friend. An equally applicable phrase is 'my pollution is your pollution'. Gases mix and even out, in concentration terms, over the entire globe. We are each our brothers' keepers. When tackling global problems, nationalist or non-cooperative policies that focus solely on the home country at the expense of other countries – beggar-thy-neighbour policies – are counterproductive.

The leading polluting nations – China (with 12,454 million tonnes and 27.51% of CO_2e), the US (with 6,673 million tonnes and 14.75%) and India (2,379 million tonnes and 6.43%) – force the rest of the world to suffer their pollution. In this way there is a huge disparity in effects between these and other heavily polluting nations and the smaller, less well-off nations. I have cited the effects of the Sahara moving southwards. The nations affected by this produce only a tiny fraction of the greenhouse gases that are destroying their ecosystems. Nigeria, the Central African Republic, Ivory Coast, Ethiopia, Ghana, Mali, Chad, Niger, Burkino Faso, Benin and Sierra Leone between them produce 1.5% of global emissions. The larger, developed nations have to develop a sensitivity to the plight of smaller, less developed nations.

The deaths caused by use of fossil fuels have economic effects on productivity, healthcare costs, labour availability, loss of skill base and general social welfare costs. Any accounting for damage has to take this loss of human life into account

It is clear from observations that the effects are getting worse over time.

A most comprehensive study was performed by a 12-person team of Chinese professors, headed by Yi-Ming Wei of the Beijing Institute of Technology. Published in the journal *Nature: Communications*,[34] the study suggests that there could be cumulative benefits of around $600 trillion by 2100, if self-preservation

34   *Nature: Communications*, vol. 11, 1624 (2020).

strategies were adopted by the nations of the world. For comparison the global GDP now is $83 trillion.

2. Assessing the costs of mitigating climate change

Chapter 8 looked at the falling costs of wind, solar and storage. These are the practical current solutions. I believe we don't have to invent other more exotic solutions. These falling costs are real. They come as a result of supportive regimes in Denmark, Germany and the US, as well as the R+D conducted by the supply chain companies. Almost all of this research has been conducted by the private sector.

This has been something of a heroic struggle for the renewables industry. Against a background of nations paying the fossil fuel industry around $400 billion in subsidies each year, wind and solar have ploughed an incredible furrow.

Subsidising pollution must stop. Why does any nation pay the polluter? Pollution kills people and puts the survival of large sections of the world's population at risk. It is backward in its thinking. I can only imagine how far we, as a species, would be advanced on the trajectory to decarbonisation if that money had been spent on researching and deploying renewable energy.

Fossil fuel subsidies come in many forms. The World Trade Organisation (WTO) has a broad definition of subsidies. It says a subsidy is any financial benefit provided by a government that gives an unfair advantage to a specific industry, business or even individual. The WTO mentions five types of subsidies:

1. Cash subsidies, such as grants

2. Tax concessions, such as exemptions, credits, or deferrals

3. Assumption of risk, such as loan guarantees

4. Government procurement policies that pay more than the free market price

5. Stock purchases that keep a company's stock price higher than market levels.

These are all considered subsidies because they reduce the cost of doing business.

Despite these subsidies, and the enormous conservative forces that exist to defend them, the cost of coal-fired generation has been estimated at 9.2 $ cents per kWh, with no charge for pollution. Wind costs between 3.5 and 6 $ cents per unit. Solar PV costs 1.5–5 $ cents.

I do not anticipate further large reductions in the costs of wind and solar. There are a few reasons for this. Until now, wind and solar have been largely connected to the grid via a network that existed before these generation technologies came along. Wind and solar developers pay only for what are called 'shallow' connections to the grid. These can be understood as local connections to the nearest grid substation that has some unused capacity to accept further electricity. These shallow connections stand in contrast to the deep connections that have to happen when all the spare shallow capacity has been used up. The Competitive Renewable Energy Zones built in Texas are an example of deep connections.

Another reason why many further price reductions will not happen has to do with the wind turbine manufacturers' lack of profitability. I have never seen, nor would I have believed, that an industry that performs such vital social, economic and environmental tasks could be so treated by the 'market'. There needs to be a fivefold increase in investments in renewable energy if the 2°C temperature threshold is to be met. There is a clear link between investment and return. Fund managers will continue to invest in fossil fuels so long as their rates of return are higher than those achieved by investing in renewables.

We have been living with market failure in the renewables industry since 2013. Markets are incapable of leading the world in the necessary social directions. During the noughties there were in the order of 15 WTG companies. They were mainly European. The non-European ones were Goldwind and Envision from China, GE from the US and Suzlon from India. There are now four European companies from whom one can buy WTGs. Their average profitability is currently less than zero.

We are in a situation where conventional economics, believing only in the short term and in competition, ignores the question of externalities. There is no hidden hand of the free market. Without government interventions we would never have had the huge deployment of renewables that led to dramatic price reductions. New rules, regulations and incentive structures were introduced by the governments mentioned above.

With bigger turbines offshore the price at which they generate electricity will continue to fall. However, a new European grid has to be built, and storage will be needed to balance the variable and intermittent nature of wind and solar. The cost of underlying technologies of DC grids and storage continues to fall. The process of developing these new technologies ought to be of extreme interest to Europe, because they are key to creating a competitive advantage for European companies. Whichever countries succeed in being first with a zero carbon electricity system will have a competitive advantage. They will, of necessity, have developed the required technologies. Local employment will increase. Exports will be assured. The leakage of currency to external fuel suppliers will have ceased, and above all the fuel will be free.

The Chinese study cited above dealt with the falling cost of sustainable technology by considering a number of scenarios. They define three levels of technological development: slow development with low decline rate of low-carbon technology costs being less than 15% every five years; medium development with medium decline rate of low carbon technology costs being 15–30% every five years; and rapid development with high decline rate of low-carbon technology costs being 30–40% every five years.

The cost of wind and solar has been declining at the latter rate for the past 10 years. For instance, with respect to offshore wind in the UK since 2014 the price of electricity delivered to the grid has gone from £150 to £117 to £58 to £40 per MWhr. When Mainstream bid on offshore wind-generated electricity into the Chilean auction in 2014, the price was $110 per MWhr In 2015 the winning bid price was $79. In 2016 Mainstream bid $41 per MWhr. We are aware of these prices because we bid into most of these auctions and, in any event, the winning bids are in the public domain.

3. Taking different levels of development into account

This issue is easier to deal with and plan for than economists have assumed. In almost all cases sustainable technologies are researched, developed and deployed in the more advanced economies. Given the rate at which China has invested in new technology R+D, it has to be included in the more developed countries.

Less developed economies more or less reap the harvest that has been planted by the richer countries. An instance of this is Mexico. Having done nothing to create the new technologies, Mexico, until recently, took full advantage of wind and solar developments elsewhere. Solar PV plants have been installed and are producing electricity at 1.5 $ cents. If coal plants had been built in place of solar the cost of electricity would have been 9.2 $ cents.

Similarly, electricity prices in Chile have been falling due to their auction system. When Mainstream first bid in 2013 our price was around 11 $ cents. In the second auction the bid price was 7.9 $ cents. In 2016 we bid 4.1 $ cents. The average price of electricity is now in the range 4–5 $ cents.

In reality, when it comes to sustainable electricity, no new policy decisions are needed for the developing world. They can just buy the cheapest power.

The problem in Africa has little to do with the available technology. Their issues are governance and corruption. We have seen attempts by western companies to build coal-fired plant in Kenya. Why would anyone invest in costly, import-heavy, coal-fired technology? This suggests that someone is gaining personally from the transaction.

Perhaps the biggest threat occurs in South East Asia. Edward Cunningham, a Harvard University specialist on China and its energy markets, points out that China is building or planning more than 300 coal plants in places as widely spread as Turkey, Vietnam, Indonesia, Bangladesh, Egypt and the Philippines. China has made more than $244 billion in energy investments abroad since 2000, much of it in recent years, according to a Boston University database. The bulk is in oil and gas, but more than $50 billion has gone towards coal. A report found that more than a quarter of coal plants under development outside China have some commitment or offer of funds from Chinese financial institutions.

I find it hard to understand why China is behaving like this. It, alone among the world powers, is the most sensitive to climate change. Some 70% of its area is semi desert, and it is hugely dependent on its great river systems. As global warming accelerates, these river systems will come under pressure. The glaciers that partially feed the rivers are reducing in size, and this will have an impact on the water available to the rivers. In addition, China has learned expensive lessons from the coal-induced pollution in its bigger cities.

The good news for those of us who think there should be no more coal-fired generation is that Vietnam is finding it very hard to fund coal-fired power stations, so its attention has turned to wind and, up to now, particularly solar PV.

4. Establishing uniform methods of accounting for each nation's contribution

There should be a level playing field across all nations. This is one of the easier conditions in any post-Paris international agreement. The world already measures the tonnages of CO_2 that each nation emits. All countries need to adopt exactly the same metrics.

China represents an example of a country committed to its own measures to reduce the carbon intensity of industrial output. In this it succeeded. However, its industrial output increased dramatically. Its targets were met yet it continued to increase CO_2 emissions. What gets measured gets managed, in business and in national budgeting. So it is of the utmost importance that the metrics are sufficient to achieve the main result, which is the reduction in, leading to the elimination of greenhouse gas emissions.

It is slightly more challenging to take accurate measurements of the emissions of natural gas at the production and distribution stages. This is partly the case because it is not in the gas companies' interests to be open with information about gas losses to the atmosphere. However, it would not be too big a stretch for nations to mandate that their gas companies accurately report on gas losses.

5. The failure of voluntarism

At the core of the design of the Paris Accord there exists a flawed architecture, which has been used by governments to resign from or otherwise thwart the agreement. The Paris Accord contains no penalties for nations that opt out, or that don't otherwise meet their targets.[35]

One of the consequences of this is the phenomenon of free riding by nations that have done nothing to reduce their emissions. They get the benefit of the efforts of complying nations without paying any price themselves. This can be quite corrosive for the populations

---

35   William Nordhaus, art. cit.

that are paying, and can lead to a popular unwillingness to continue paying that price. The Paris Accord is just one in a series of failed attempts stretching back to COP 1 in 1995. They have been 'undermined by myopic or venal leaders who have no interest in long-term global issues and refuse to take the problem seriously'.[36]

Paris, like Kyoto before it, has failed. Modelling has suggested that global emissions would need to decline by about 3% annually in the coming years for the world to limit warming to the 2°C target. Actual emissions have grown by about 2% annually over the last two decades.

William Nordhaus's article 'The Climate Club'[37] deserves to be considered by governments at the postponed COP 26 in Glasgow. He proposes the establishment of a club of nations that commit to systematically reducing their emissions. They agree mitigation measures, and give one another targets. They introduce carbon taxes that are large enough to motivate companies and homeowners to change their behaviour.

Not all countries will want to be members of the club. Free riding by these countries will be avoided by erecting tariff barriers between club members and non-club members. This arrangement would have to be relatively simple to understand and police. Instead of estimating the carbon content of products coming from non-club members and allowing in compliant products, it would be much simpler to place a tariff on all products. This would be a severe imposition on all non-club members. It would lead to pressure from exporters in the non-club on their native governments. Downward pressure on their GDPs and unemployment would be a consequence.

Replacing all fossil-fired generation involves upfront investment. It is appropriate to enquire why this is so, if the main strategy is to build cheaper renewable generating plant. Studies carried out by Mainstream staff indicate that 900,000MW

36 Ibid.
37 Ibid.

of new wind-generation plant will have to be built offshore. Approximately the same amount of solar PV will have to be built around the Mediterranean basin. So although the cost of the final green electricity will be cheaper than coal- or gas-fired generation the system costs of decarbonisation will involve capital investment in the following areas:

- building new grids;

- building sufficient generation to replace fossils used in transport and heating;

- installing sufficient electricity storage capacity to cope with the variability of wind and solar;

- building new hydrolysers to replace hydrogen produced from natural gas, for use as a chemical feedstock;

- investing in sufficient R+D to produce cheaper storage, hydrolysers, purpose-built shipping, upgrading of ports and, especially, grids.

The investment in climate mitigation strategies is complicated by the fact that solutions have to be found for the huge overhang of debt resulting from Covid-19 expenditures. Instead of one large quantity of money that has to be found to repay the Covid-19 debt, climate mitigation investments have to be provided for as well. Printing money carries added inflation risks, and will not be seen by many governments as a possible tactic.

It could be argued that the Covid pandemic occupies a category of risk and expenditure that has to be dealt with immediately. It is a health expenditure that is more extreme than any other health cost that has been encountered to date. However, there will be a cure, or at least a series of medicines that will allow sufferers to function somewhat normally.

At the time of writing, there are 239 Covid vaccines in development around the world, of which 45 are now in clinical testing, with 10 in use. The work to develop them happened in record time, thanks to an unprecedented pace of innovation, scientific ingenuity and global collaboration.

Mutations of the virus are currently worrying governments and their populations, but over 80 million people around the world have already had their jabs, with Israel and the UK among the countries leading the race. Furthermore, scientists are confident that vaccines will at least lessen the effects of the virus mutations, and that the vaccines can be tweaked to account for them.

We should remind ourselves that TB, smallpox, polio, measles, flu and bubonic and pneumonic plague epidemics have been largely dealt with in the sense that they don't cause an economic upset such as has been experienced with Covid. Even malaria, probably the major killer for which there is no antidote, has been eliminated from Italy, for instance. Humankind will find a way to deal with Covid. In this sense it is a non-systemic occurrence. It must be dealt with immediately, and I believe it will be. A series of one-off investments, however large they may be, is necessary. The infrastructure exists to deliver a solution. There are many large pharma companies, brilliantly equipped labs, scanning electron microscopes, tens of thousands of well-educated researchers, a well-trodden testing methodology for new drugs, and a transparent regulatory environment. Of equal importance is the motivation to find a cure or an antidote. High profits will accrue to the company that finds the solution.

Unlike what happens with global warming, there is no section of humanity that will lie and spend billions to try and stop this research.

Climate change, however, is systemic. We are in a once-off transition to sustainability for which there is no precedence or infrastructure. The regulatory environment is a shambles, as is evidenced by the failure of both the Kyoto Protocol and the Paris Accord. Whereas pharma companies are profitable, the companies that provide the main solutions to climate change struggle with lack of profits. The reason for this is that with renewable energy, whose fuel is free and whose marginal cost is zero, the price of electricity falls. The companies that provide renewable energy sell into a marketplace where the price falls in proportion to the amount of renewable energy available. Customers gain and many of the solutions providers have gone out of business.

The theoretical solutions are there, but there is a lack of imagination in putting the solution package together. I believe the Nordhaus 'Climate Club' idea is a vital component of the solution. We rely on our politicians to put the regulatory environment in place. They are the people who have to articulate the solution and sell it to their voters, but so far they have been unable to do this. To a greater or lesser extent they live in the past.

If we revert to the groundbreaking work of Professor Wei's Chinese committee we notice that they advance compelling macro-economic arguments which should help politicians to paint a sustainable future. They say that if we agree on self-preserving national solutions the cumulative benefit to the world will be more than $600 trillion by 2100. If we continue with current plans (national defined contributions – NDCs) the world will be worse off to the extent of $700 trillion. This 'policy as usual' proposition probably implies the collapse of civilisation.

To accomplish any major change, there have to be incentives to do the right thing, as well as disincentives for persisting with current destructive behaviour. I am convinced that putting a tax on CO_2 emissions can provide the required disincentive. Such a carbon tax must be at a level that will encourage polluters to change behaviour. We have seen a low level of tax operate in Europe. We have seen companies finding easy ways to dodge these low-level taxes, buying carbon credits from Russia at knock-down prices. They were also allowed grandfathering rights, which bizarrely put a value on pollution credits. I recall that at the time the emission trading scheme was introduced in 2005 the balance sheets of polluters were enhanced by these credits. By comparison, the balance sheet of Airtricity, which caused no pollution, was unaffected, so we were placed at a competitive disadvantage as against polluters.

The higher the level of tax the quicker will be the transition to sustainability, and speed is of the essence now.

It is quite fitting that the 'polluter pays' principle be applied, but the money generated should be ring-fenced and used to implement the decarbonisation agenda. One of the desired outcomes of a carbon tax would be the provision of funds to which solution providers had access. If we want to accelerate the transition we need stronger, better-capitalised and more profitable solution providers.

There are some areas where the technology is proven and is cheap, like wind, solar PV and lithium ion battery storage. They are also getting cheaper. However, one area needs R+D funding, and that is grids. Most future wind energy will emanate from the near seas and oceans of Northern Europe. Solar should be made where it is cheaper, and that is around the Mediterranean basin. These two great resources need to be linked, and connected to the centres of population. Currently the design of future grids is left in the hands of national grid monopolists. The planning document of their representative association, ENTSO-E, for 2050 shows no offshore wind farms or connections between solar and northern wind.

The money raised by taxing polluters can be used in a number of ways. The living standards of poorer sections of society have to be protected, and some of the carbon tax can be used for this purpose. Early stage R+D can be funded, since up to a technology readiness level of 4 to 5 is relatively cheap, and social returns on focused R+D can be high. A proportion of the carbon tax has to find its way to the wind and solar solution providers. Instead of just being paid for electricity, manufacturers and developers should be paid for pollution abatement as well.

However, on a global scale, capital expenditures to bring about the transition will reach high levels. I have made an attempt to evaluate them in this table:

Continent/Country	Population in 2050	Renewable MW to be built			Cost	New grids
		WIND	SOLAR	NUCLEAR		
	MILION	GW	GW	GW	$ TRILLION	$ TRILLION
Europe all	710	1340	1340	0.120	2.73	0.91
China 100% Europe GDP	1,402	10.262	10.262	58	20.856	6.952
China ½ Europe	1,402	5.132	5.132	58	10.428	3.476
USA + Canada	430	3,635	4,038	88.2	7.891	2.63
India	1,639	8,367,	11.196	5.4	14.282	5.71
Rest of Asia, minus Japan etc.	2072	11.718	7.812	.045	19.575	6.525
Japan, Korea, Taiwan	177	1.267	2.111	0	1.681	0.56
Africa	2,490	176.9	206.43	0	0.280	.093
Latam (Latin America) including Central America + Caribbean	760	4638	6184	0	7.73	2.58
Oceania	60	.27	.45	0	0.5	0.16
Total	9740					
Total spend if China GDP is 100% Europe					75.165	22.727
50% Europe					64.737	19.251

Assumptions:

1. China, if it grows at 6% per annum, can reach EU per capita GDP in 23 years, well within the 2050 time period.

2. The cost of wind is projected at $1 million per megawatt.

3. The cost of solar is projected at $0.5 million per megawatt.

4. In its November 2016 report, *Capital Cost Estimates for Utility Scale Electricity Generation Plants*, the US Energy Information Administration (EIA) calculated that, in constant 2002 values, the realised output of a nuclear power plant built in the US grew from $1500/kW in the 1960s to $5945/kW.

5. Population and GDP per head are the main drivers of the quantity of generating plant needed.

6. Europe would have to replace 75% of its nuclear fleet by 2050.

7. The overall nuclear fleet remains the same in Europe.

8. In the US 60% of renewable energy build will be by wind, at a capacity factor of 50%, and by solar, to supply 40% of renewable energy at a capacity factor of 30%.

9. Nuclear plant remains the same in the US, but 90% has to be rebuilt.

10. Canada and the US are lumped together – 82% of Canada is supplied by hydro + nuclear, so they were left out of the equation.

11. The Indian economy grows at 4% per year for 30 years, and electricity follows this 100%.

12. The Brookings institute has estimated that electricity in India will grow at 6.2% until 2030. I have assumed 5% until 2050.

13. I have assumed that the growth rate in Africa will be a mere 2% per year.

There is no provision in this table for electricity storage, an apparently serious omission that requires some explanation.

Most countries are at an early stage in investing in renewables. At these early stages no storage is necessary. Countries such as Ireland (at 40% penetration) and Denmark (at 50%) have got to these levels of renewable generation without the need for storage. When the various countries get to the stage of needing storage, the price will be very different from what it is now. In addition, the lithium ion storage solution may not be the cheapest or most effective when the global demand for utility scale takes off.

A large figure has been included for grids in the above table. However, grids are more than just wires that transport electricity. They allow balancing of supply and demand. For example, a large storm tracks across Ireland, coming from the Atlantic. Without the Supergrid the only country that benefits from the wind energy is Ireland. There could be a shortage of electricity in Germany and Poland at the same time that Ireland is being oversupplied. Without the Supergrid, there will always be this imbalance.

The Supergrid provides another balancing service. The sun shines strongest in the northern hemisphere in summer, when the wind is at its weakest. By linking up the Mediterranean with Northern Europe, high sun balances low wind in summer. The opposite happens in winter.

Yet another way the Supergrid helps balance electricity supply is by capturing a storm along its path. Instead of successive peaks occurring in the countries along the length of the storm, a more even profile of renewable generation happens.

The Supergrid is also needed because the major resource is offshore in Europe and around the Mediterranean basin. These need to be connected to one another and to centres of population.

It is not possible to cost electricity storage in the above table, because the extent and scope of the Supergrid is not determined as yet.

Without the Supergrid there would have to be a massive overbuild of renewable generation plant in each country, accompanied by a large installation of local storage. Even with large quantities of local storage, some countries (possibly up to 10 in Europe) don't have enough local renewable generation, even if it were to be fully exploited.

We do know that by the time storage becomes a limiting factor in the roll-out of renewable energy, its cost will have fallen hugely from where it is at the moment. Up to now the cost has been falling by 18% per year. With the acceleration of the deployment of battery electric vehicles (BEVs) and the greatly increased demand for batteries that follows from this, I see no reason why this cost-reducing trend will not continue.

BEVs represent a great change in the energy world. They replace the internal combustion engine (ICE). The use of primary energy (refined crude oil) in an ICE, while serving humanity well, made use of only 16–21% of the chemical energy in the oil. When electricity is used in BEVs 90% of the electricity that is stored in the batteries is used to drive the vehicle, so the use of energy reduces when vehicles are powered by electricity. In the US transport accounts for 28% of primary energy, while in EU 28 transport accounted for 30.8%. there is a reduction in the overall energy requirement in proportion to the number of BEVs used for transport. One fifth of the energy currently required for transport would be needed if electricity were to be used. More energy would be saved than the entire current production of electricity.

There can be no transition without transmission. However, on the positive side, with adequate transmission, which means the Supergrid, there is every chance of being able to accomplish decarbonisation.

CHAPTER 19

Where I'm At Now

There were times in my life when I wished I was like other boys I was friendly with. They were happy with the current state of affairs, and I was always wanting to change things. I suppose this could be called a neurotic disposition, and until I got older I thought it was. Some time in my 20s I began to realise that this internal force to which I was subject could be very useful in solving problems. I encountered many situations at work where things were clearly broken and took great pleasure in fixing them. Innovation was central to nearly all my solutions.

I enjoyed my time at university enormously. I was very serious, full of enthusiasm to better the lot of the students and, indeed, the world around me. I played few games and was preoccupied with student politics. It was in college that I became aware of the 'jolly rugby types'. By and large they couldn't care less about Vietnam, racial discrimination or any of the burning issues of the day. They loved playing rugby. It slowly dawned on me that they were having fun, and that that was a great thing. The question 'Why don't you have fun as well?' stole up on me, and so I started playing rugby very late in life. In hindsight it is amazing that I came through Blackrock College, the premier rugby school, without hardly touching a rugby ball. It also speaks of how useless I was at the game. I surely would have been pressed into action if I had shown any ability at all.

I rectified all that when I left UCD and joined the ranks of the jolly rugby types. It's a great team game. I don't believe that there is any other game where one relies on one's team-mates quite so much. It's a game where even relatively unathletic types like me can participate and even win sometimes.

I'd go training twice a week and play a match at weekends. In 1971, although no longer a student, I played with UCD and we won the Third Cs cup in Leinster. Later, in 1977, having joined the Lansdowne Club, I captained the Third As to win our division cup that year. That was great. Then, when I was transferred within the ESB to work in County Mayo, I was on the Ballina RFC team that won the senior Connacht cup, and we weren't even in the first division at the time. Lansdowne, of which I am still a member, is a great club. I made many friends there and am delighted to say they are still strong friends.

* * *

My introduction to fishing came when I was about six years of age. In our house in Elphin, County Roscommon, I recall coming down one morning and finding a pail full of bloody water and about three pike. My father had caught them while out fishing with a buddy the night before. I remember they had ferocious teeth and I was never sure whether the blood was of human or fish origin. That incident, far from deterring me, whetted my appetite for fishing. Later on, when we were living in Monaghan, my father used to bring the family fishing on Lake Muckno in Castleblayney. We used to catch perch and pike. From then on, any time I had the opportunity I would spend some time fishing.

I once caught 10 salmon in one day on the River Moy at Foxford, County Mayo. I once caught a 9-kg salmon on the worm at Foxford. This was a specimen fish.

Fishing the Abhann Mór at Bangor Erris is a great treat. We are only allowed to fly-fish on this river. It is one of the rivers in which the salmon numbers have been going down for the past 30 years. It has still not reduced to the level of the Slaney, or other Irish rivers. In 2019 I caught a 5.5-kg salmon there.

When we lived in Crossmolina, which is on the upper shore of Lough Conn, I used to own a small rowing boat. Lough Conn has only wild trout, and I spent many days and evenings hunting them. The boat was made of fibreglass, which was a bit of a rarity around Lough Conn in those days. The other fishermen thought it was too flimsy and one day I had to disabuse them of that notion by grinding a small stone to sand using the oar.

Fishing in the tropics is a wonderful experience. Tropical fish tend to be stronger than cold-water fish from the northern seas. Bone fish is one variety – although it weighs less than 1.5 kg it can run for 100 meters – you would cut your finger badly if you tried to hold the line while the fish is running. The bigger varieties of tropical fish, such as the tarpon and permit, are very hard to catch. One fishes for them with flies and very strong rods. Most fishing is done in water that varies in depth from 30 to 60 centimetres. The boat has a platform at the end on which the guide stands and punts the boat along with a 6-metre pole. He sees the fish first and instructs the fisherman where to land the fly. In Cuba in 2019 we were punting along when the guide told us a school of three tarpon was approaching. His instruction was '40 feet, 11 o'clock, then strip'. The fly resembles a shrimp, and when you strip the fly hops along the bottom, mimicking a shrimp's behaviour. The tarpon took the fly and ran uncontrollably around the boat for the next 50 minutes. We eventually landed him. He weighed 45.5 kg. We released him quickly, having taken a photograph. This was the only tarpon I have ever landed.

On another occasion we were fishing in a deeper pool where we could see there were fish flashing. A small 4-kg tarpon took the fly and began a run across this long pool. Suddenly an enormous black and red shape emerged from the depths and attacked the hooked tarpon. All I got back was a cut line. The tarpon, fly and line all seemed to have been eaten by the monster. Our guide explained that a cubera snapper had done the evil deed.

I fished a few times for Pacific salmon off the Queen Charlotte Islands off the coast of British Columbia. They are now called the Haida Gwaii, the original native name for the islands. Here the technique is called mooching. The head of a frozen herring is cut off at an angle. Two hooks are embedded in the flesh and it is trawled behind the boat at the depth we think the fish are feeding. There are five species of Pacific salmon – the chinook or spring fish is the largest, and have been caught up to 40 kg. The others are the sockeye, coho, chum and pink. There are colonies of giant sea lions on some of the near offshore rocky outcroppings. They cannot catch or even eat salmon normally. However, if the salmon is hooked at the end of a fishing line, the awkward sea lion can grab the salmon. It has happened to me a few times. The sea lions' teeth are unable to cut the salmon so they bash it to pieces on rocks. On one occasion I had a bald eagle grab and make off with a salmon I was reeling in.

Fishing is incredibly relaxing. There is no time to think of work or anything else; you just concentrate on where to land the fly and how to play the fish. Some people, including my father, consider that fishing with a rod and line is a waste of time, for which patience is needed. So, even though he introduced me to fishing, he didn't do much of it himself.

* * *

For me sleeping at lunchtime is a life-saver and I grab some sleep every lunchtime – in the office, or out in my car if I'm elsewhere. It's been a habit since an episode in my 20s, when I was worried about feeling weak after a rugby training session. I went for a medical check and the doctor said my blood pressure was a bit high, so I had further tests but nothing showed up. The doctor inquired what I did at lunchtime. I explained I usually did fitness training for rugby. 'Why don't you sleep?' he asked, adding that that's what he did every day. And it's what I've done almost every day since. Even when all that nonsense was going on in BNM, I always made sure that I could sleep because I had to get through that one way or the other and emerge on the far side without too much damage. It means I always have a lot of energy in the afternoon and avoid the mid-afternoon slump that other people talk about and that I noticed in myself in college.

My long-time PA, Marian Shanahan, jokes that my lunchtime routine shows how for some things I am a creature of habit.

* * *

I've always enjoyed participating in sport and kept up team games for as long as I could. I still play golf. On my return to Dublin from Mayo, I went back to playing at Lansdowne for a bit, until a memorable match against students from Maynooth College in County Kildare. I was in my late 30s, as were many of my team-mates, and the opposing players were about half our age. Having a considerable weight advantage, we were able to push them around the place in scrums, but running was an issue. Late in the match the students scored a try which, if they converted, they would win. If not, the match would go to extra time. I remember hoping the kicker would convert it, but he missed. We got beaten in the extra time that followed. I was sitting in the dressing room for 10 minutes afterwards, totally shattered, not even able to undo my laces, so I knew it was time to call it a day on rugby.

I started playing indoor soccer instead, which I did until I was well into my 40s, and I loved it. A group of us, ex-Lansdowne people, played five-a-side on Sunday mornings in the Ballybrack indoor five-a side court. I used to bring Robert and Lesley and they could run about perfectly safely. It was a great release for me at the end of the week when I was working at BNM. I would come off the course saturated with sweat and utterly relaxed.

Now it's the gym and golf. I have all kinds of physical problems from my rugby days and had to have back surgery in my 50s. I do stretching exercises every day when I get up, which help with my back and my neck. I play golf mainly out of the Powerscourt Club in Enniskerry, County Wicklow, and also Elm Park in Dublin 4, although I find that a bit tight. I am also a five-day member of Portmarnock in Dublin, where the links course is magnificent.

Hildegarde and I would often walk around Dublin Bay at weekends. If I had time I would cycle more because I love to cycle. I bought a bike, mainly to strengthen my knee before and after a knee replacement operation. I remember doing cartwheels at Lansdowne Road during training in 1977 and doing something to my knee. I then tried to ski on it and really pranged it. When you get an injury like that, it comes back at you and it is a site for arthritis to develop.

I've always been fit but I wouldn't dream of doing a marathon and putting my body through all that pounding on the road. I just love exercise for the fun of it – having fun is a big component of what I do in life. Life is about living and having a great time as well as creating all sorts of interesting things.

* * *

One of my great pleasures in life now is travelling to Chicago to take part in the 'Bike Beer Blast'. I was introduced to the Blasters by Rory Smith, my old friend from rugby days and a graduate of De Paul University. With other graduates of his alma mater, we cycle from there to Lake Michigan, stopping off at various pubs along the way. The first pub is Pog Mo Hone, where jugs of fine beer are happily quaffed. We usually cool off by swimming in Lake Michigan before eating very American hamburgers.

I have some great friends who don't appreciate food. It is for them an energy provider, something that one has to do but which represents a waste of precious time. I cannot imagine what life would be like if I didn't enjoy eating. It is one of the great harmless pleasures in life.

I enjoy eating out and drinking fine wine but I hardly drink spirits at all. If you go to Scotland, they're keen for you to try their single malts. I am kind of fascinated by whisky drinkers. Wine is what you drink with a meal and always seems very civilised; beer is what you drink when you're out to 'drink', and whiskey is something you do after the meal. I remember my father coming in from a round of golf and having one glass of Redbreast Irish whiskey. He would ask for water and put in three or four drops 'to release the aroma'. He reminded me many times that it was potentially fatal to water another man's whiskey, at least in the old Western movies he loved.

I have a wine cellar, and that is the only thing I invest in. I don't invest in property and Hildegarde and I have lived for decades in the same house in Clonskeagh, Dublin. However, I think I'll enlarge my wine cellar and put in a small section for whiskeys (and perhaps whiskies). I'll probably learn how to drink it because it seems to be such a fascinating kind of subject – all these guys can't be wrong. Certainly, my father loved it, sitting sipping his Redbreast for ages. I am more into volume myself!

Travel is like a drug for me. The idea of sitting in a plane 35,000 feet above the ground, eating good food and being served fine wine is one of my ideas of heaven. The concept of heavier-than-air machines travelling through the skies never ceases to amaze me. I am constantly amazed when I see a Boeing 747 or an Airbus A 380 taking off. Because they are so big they seem to be almost stationary, whereas they are flying at 300 kilometres per hour. The modern airframe and wings are constructed of carbon fibre and glue. Where can the triumph of man be better exemplified than with these modern B787s and Airbus A350s? Held together by glue, more comfortable and causing less jet-lag than the last generation of airplanes.

Covid-19 has put paid to flying for a while. I know only one thing. I will be visiting faraway places when flying is allowed again.

Conclusion

The changes that the average person in the developed world has experienced during the past century are challenging even to list. We have conquered many of the difficulties that nature routinely throws at us. Motor cars, planes, antibiotics, transport of goods, computers, robots, fertilisers, 100% electrification, contraception, the enfranchisement and liberation of women, materials science, health diagnostics, social media, digitalisation, information storage and psychological insights are just some of the breakthroughs that have freed the majority of the people of the developed world from short lives of crushing drudgery.

These developments were accomplished by a world population that amounted, on average, to less than half today's global population. The rate of creation of new knowledge can be assessed by looking at the increase in the number of PhD students over the last century. In 1900 there were 365 PhD students in US universities. In 1990 there were 38,238. Some estimates put the current number close to 100,000. China is the world leader in the production of PhDs, outnumbering the US on an annual basis for the first time in 2008. By then, the Asian giant had awarded more than 240,000 doctorates since 1978, when PhD programmes, stopped during the Cultural Revolution, were reinstated. A mere 18 students enrolled for doctorates in 1978, but since then enrolment has expanded by 24% annually.

The number of PhD students is just one measure of how quickly new knowledge is being created. An enormous amount of research is being carried out outside the academic sphere, by companies, independent think-tanks and government agencies.

The future is uncharted territory. It will be constructed out of collective cultural, scientific and technological discoveries. The pace of change is accelerating as the body of knowledge increases. Knowledge is a positive force in the ongoing march of our species. It is not only in the area of hard science that knowledge builds. In the soft sciences of psychology, cultural studies, anthropology and economics new knowledge is being built at a rate similar to or even greater than that being achieved in the hard sciences. We will see astonishing change over the course of the 21st century.

Science and technology will continue to expand the human knowledge base. Inroads will continue to be made into the secrets as yet unrevealed about the human body, the cosmos and viruses, to name just a few.

The rest of the world will have to accommodate itself to the new reality that China is now the largest world power and will continue to grow economically at a spectacular rate compared to other countries. This growth is based on the rapid deployment of the most modern innovations in every sphere of economic activity. It was reported in November 2020 that China had installed 700,000 5G base stations, as against 10,000 in the US. A total of 10,000,000 5G base stations will be built in China, 2,000,000 of them in 2021–23. We have seen Europe lose its lead in the transmission of electricity to the Chinese. Both ABB and Siemens invented the DC circuit-breaker, only to have it built and deployed in China. The Chinese are facing up to the decarbonisation of energy in a better planned way than any other country. Unless the EU meets the challenge of basing electricity generation on non-dispatchable energy sources, we will cede the development, manufacture and sale of this necessary range of products to China.

'What does the future hold?' is a valid question. It is perhaps more pertinent to ask 'What *must* the future hold if we want our species to continue to thrive?'

The area in which the real hope for humanity resides is in tackling global warming. The Earth has one atmosphere. A tonne of CO_2 released into it in Dublin is mixed and diluted and gets dispersed everywhere. Molecules of this CO_2 will be found over Beijing, Canberra and Santiago. We have to come together, as people of the world, to eliminate carbon emissions.

What was accomplished at Paris in 2015 was momentous. Although it has failed so far to live up to expectations, possibilities arise that otherwise would not have. The upcoming COP 26 in Glasgow can begin the change process that will lead to concrete steps to eliminate the emissions of CO_2.

What gives rise to this hope rests on the political will of the leading nations. China has committed to carbon neutrality by 2060. The EU has launched a similar initiative and has allocated a €1 trillion budget to greening energy in the immediate future. US President Joe Biden has appointed the vastly experienced John Kerry to head up the US climate change group.

Biden brought up climate change in the televised debates with Trump in the lead-up to the 2020 presidential election, nailing his colours to the mast in front of the biggest audience possible, and now has a mandate to undertake what is needed to fight the war on climate change. He has proposed a sweeping $2 trillion clean-energy plan, with a goal of making the electric grid emissions-free by 2035 and reaching an economy-wide net-zero emissions target just 15 years later.

And what of the bulk of humanity that has yet to experience the enhanced life experience that all the advances in science, business, technology and appropriate political representation already offer to advanced societies?

I fall into the camp of those who see a greatly enhanced experience for the majority of our species in the future. One of the reasons I am hopeful has to do with the explosive increase in knowledge. I see parallels between the Catholic Church's suppression of the scientific discoveries of Galileo and Copernicus and the modern rejection of the science of global warming. In both cases the denial of science has to do with its interference with the power of dominant, fundamentally conservative forces in society. The Catholic Church of the Middle Ages promulgated a self-serving view of the world, one in which it decided what was real, and what wasn't. The Church's interpretation of the Old and New Testaments provided the rationale for their orthodoxy. Being the perceived font of all knowledge enabled it to impose its power and extract wealth. The rejection of the fact that the Earth is a globe that revolves around the sun is mirrored today by the oil industry's rejection of global warming, aided and abetted by the Trump administration of 2016–20.

I find it hard to imagine what life will be like in 100 years, never mind 2,000. Of course, for the overwhelming majority of us it really doesn't matter, as we won't be around to see it. However, notwithstanding the fact of our mortality, it seems to me that most of us would love to be able to anticipate an orderly evolution of our species.

What is it that we are evolving to?

There must be a more equal distribution of the wealth of the world, as between the emerging – including the tribal – world, and the developed world. The hard and soft sciences come together here. We need to greatly increase our understanding of anthropology, and the transition from tribal society to modern state.

None of the innovations we have seen in, for example, medicine and technology, will materially affect the deep anthropological structures that underpin human nature. I see very little to suggest that the species has evolved in any material way during the last three millennia. The writings of Confucius are as relevant today as when they were written in the Analects. The Judeo-Christian value set is still a good guide to values.

According to those who have studied the emergence of early man, evolution happens in response to environmental changes, particularly so when those changes threaten human reproduction. So long as the basic earthly environment remains roughly as it is I think human nature will remain basically the same. I say this based on the similarities between ancient, medieval and contemporary writing. Art, which holds up a mirror to nature, may have changed as new tools and techniques became available, but it still depicts recognisable human attributes.

Our greatest crisis is the build-up of CO_2 in the atmosphere and the havoc it wreaks. This can largely be solved, even with the technology to hand today. The Paris Accord has to be given teeth, and sufficient funds need to be allocated for the creation of an alternative sustainable energy future. Without it I see little prospect for our great-grandchildren.

In many parts of this book I have demonstrated that we have the technology to deal with most of the issues that decarbonisation throws up. Markets themselves have their true limitations shown up when it comes to dealing with decarbonisation. There is no unseen hand of a benign market force at work. We currently spend $350 billion a year globally on installing carbon-free electricity generation. That spend needs to be increased six- or seven-fold.

Electricity consumption is a mere 14–20% of the overall energy needs, depending on the country. The remaining 80–86% relies heavily on oil and gas. Transport and heating have to be tackled if decarbonisation is to be realised. Decarbonisation also means that fossil-heavy chemical feedstock has to be decarbonised. Hydrogen and ammonia (NH_3) are made from natural gas at the moment, with 70 million tonnes of hydrogen consumed globally each year, resulting in an annual emission of 830 million tonnes of CO_2.

There is no substitute for hydrogen as a chemical feedstock, at least in the short term. It is expensive to manufacture, but it is technically feasible. Water (H_2O) can be separated into its constituents, but there is a 30% loss of energy during this process, called hydrolysis.

Electricity can supply almost all of our future energy needs. Renewables are now able to supply power more cheaply than coal, oil, gas and nuclear. Wind and solar have collapsed in price over the past 15 years. Price digression still continues. I was surprised to see the results of the recent Portuguese auction, which resulted in a price of 1.4 $ cents per unit of electricity. This price should be available around the Mediterranean basin, and throughout desert latitudes, where solar radiation is at its strongest. Offshore wind has seen equally dramatic price reductions. Shell bid 3.96 pence (sterling) per unit of electricity for power in the North Sea in 2019. An indication of just how quickly the price has fallen can be seen in the Mainstream bid of 11.4 pence in 2016.

Innovation is playing a key role in wind and solar manufacture. The larger the wind turbine the cheaper the electricity, for the same wind speed. In 30 years the size of turbines has gone from 0.25MW to 12MW, a factor of 48, but turbines aren't 48 times bigger. They are perhaps five times bigger: taller towers, longer blades, stronger foundations. The cost is proportional to the amount of material used, whereas the output is proportional to the length of the blade squared. On this basis we will continue to see even bigger turbines, perhaps reaching 20–25MW by 2030. At sea there is no limit on the size of blade and tower that can be brought to site.

There is no doubt that human ingenuity can solve almost any problem that we encounter today. However, there are certain limits relating to the laws of physics that impose themselves. For instance, the speed of light is a given, and it is not possible for anything to travel any faster. In a sphere less known to the general public are the laws of thermodynamics. If a process of combustion is involved in supplying energy, there are inevitable inefficiencies. For instance the most efficient combined-cycle gas turbine operates at a conversion rate of 60% of the inherent energy in the gas into useful energy. The internal combustion engine (ICE) operates at a conversion rate of 20%. It is for this reason that the current Klondike-like rush into hydrogen is set to fail. To be a useful source of power, hydrogen has to be burned in an ICE, or otherwise chemically manipulated in a fuel cell, with 50% efficiency at best. If the raw electricity is used to drive an electric motor in a car or a lorry the efficiency is 90%. There is also a loss of 30% when converting wind- or solar-generated electricity into hydrogen by electrolysis, as well as the capital investment in the equipment to do this.

Electrification based on wind, solar, geothermal, waste combustion and nuclear is the necessary precondition to decarbonisation and the removal of the threat of global warming.

However, electricity needs to be transported from where it can be generated to where the populations live. By and large this transport system doesn't exist and will have to be built. It is the greatest logistical challenge of our age. I have proposed the Supergrid as the solution. In a world consuming 250% of the electricity that is consumed today the need for the Supergrid is up there with the great challenges facing the engineering, scientific and business communities.

To this end I have set up SuperNode (see page 163). It is the greatest challenge I have faced, but one that I truly relish. I hope that before the end of the 2020s, SuperNode will offer the total logistical solution to complete decarbonisation.

THANK YOU

I would like to thank John Lavery who insisted that the book get written, to the late and great Brendan Halligan who kept pushing me in the same direction, to Sheila Wayman and to the editor Fiona Biggs.

To all my work colleagues whose innovations had a large part to play with the successful outcomes that we achieved.

To Garry O'Sullivan and the Currach Books team for all their help and advice.